NAIL SALONS

WOMEN & ENTREPRENEURSHIP

Nail salons are a "Great topic about something so commonplace we typically don't consider its origins, operations or outcome," a reviewer noted.

Did you know that some nail salons provide childcare? Some nail salons provide Champagne. Some nail salons provide both services. Who knew? There is a lot to learn about nail salons!

The story begins in the fiery backdrop of the 1975 Vietnam War then brings us current in America and around the world.

We meet two refugee women who were among the first licensed Vietnamese manicurists in the United States. They explain their experiences with actress Tippi Hedren and tell why she was named the "Godmother" of the nail salon business.

At last we get to hear the opinions and experiences of manicurists.

In *Nail Salons* customers share Rants Raves and Reviews of service expectations and service delivery. One customer raved "You don't come to the Four Seasons Spa for cutting-edge polish colors or wacky lacquers. You come to drop a shoe size! ...and then leave with hands and feet of a newborn!"

Nail Salons is a bestseller, a *tell-all* and a *must-read* for every customer and manicurist.

LayDee Publishing
P.O. Box 1307
Ocean Shores, WA 98569
USA
www.nailsalonsbook.com

© Copyright 2014 by Claudette Varnado. All rights reserved. Manufactured and printed in the United States.
Bulk Orders: www.nailsalonsbook.com
Cover: PixelStudio
Interior Design: Delaney-
Designs Price $18.00 USD

ISBN-13: 978-0-692-34366-1

First Edition 2015

Note: Web addresses or links contained in this book may change or become invalid after publication of this book due to the dynamic nature of the Internet.

ISBN 978-0-692-34366-1

9 780692 343661 >

NAIL SALONS

"THE TRUE STORY
OF THE LITTLEST BIG BUSINESS"

Claudette Varnado

DEDICATION

I would like to sincerely thank my sisters Izola Etter and Dianna Varnado for their encouragement. I'd like to thank Fahizah Alim, Ann Bock and Kathleen Wolgemuth for their constructive feed-back and guidance. I'd also like to give special thanks to Thuan Le, Dr. Tam Nguyen and Becky Hambelton for sharing photographs and personal stories. I'm also grateful for the personal stories and cooperation of Kien Nguyen, Lynn's Nails, Linh Nguyen, Yen Rist, Monique Nguyen and Hieu Ngo. Many thanks also to the Vietnamese, Cambodian, Hmong and Laotian students who shared their experiences and started me on my journey to this end.

Claudette Varnado

CONTENTS

INTRODUCTION

In 1975, fate led one woman, actress Tippi Hedren, to help 20 Vietnamese women learn the skill of manicuring. It was not easy. It took Tippi Hedren's glamour, sincerity, wisdom and foresight to persuade the 20 skeptical immigrant women to learn the manicuring trade. They in turn taught other women the skill. Women helped women. Despite their war-torn refugee background and inability to speak English, they persevered. Through their efforts they unwittingly laid the foundation for America's 8-billion-dollar nail care industry. Through self-employment in nail salons, these female entrepreneurs earned money and were thus empowered to lift up their families, communities and ultimately their adopted nation.

In *Nail Salons* true story, there are several important people who like Tippi Hedren played major contributing roles in the formative years of the inception and development of the nail industry. For instance, Thuan Le and Yen Rist who contribute throughout this book are two of the first Vietnamese manicurists in the United States. They describe their refugee experiences, their association with Tippi Hedren and their subsequent nail care careers. Beauty college owners Becky and Charles Hambelton and Minh and Kien Nguyen also played significant roles in the ultimate success story.

As a result of the actions of these individuals and the resilience and tenacity of the legions of female entrepreneurs who followed in their path, the Vietnamese nail salon was born. It is an ethnic niche and an international cultural icon. It is one of America's greatest beauty exports.

While there are few books about the iconic nail salon, numerous comedy skits have appeared. A now famous skit was performed by Anjelah Johnson. In it she mimics an Asian manicurist persuad-ing her customer to up-grade the basic service price. The skit has received 17 million views on YouTube.

Some people think the skit is hilarious. Some manicurists think the skit is inaccurate and even racist. Vietnamese-American co-medienne Dat Phan likes to poke fun at nail salons in his routines. So do others. Miley Cyrus also recently performed in a (2013) comedy skit with Jimmy Fallon. In it she plays a bumbling manicur-ist in a salon.

However, it is no joke that in America Vietnamese-owned nail salons hold a dominant 51% share of the nail services sector. Interestingly, 96% of nail salons are owned by Vietnamese females. Like McDonalds's and Starbucks Vietnamese nail salons are familiar sights on most streets. Yet, their aggregate economic significance flies under the radar of Big Business industry observers.

These small businesses provide self-employment and jobs which infuse big money into local, national and international economies. The dynamic industry growth from this retail services sector has in turn stimulated product development in nail polishes, files, clip-pers and nippers and other tools used in the trade. This growth required that distribution and manufacturing sectors expand. In America, over 400 manufacturers have appeared in just the last 20 years. As a result, more and more jobs were created.

In addition to the industry's dynamic economic impact, there is an explosive cultural impact in the United States and abroad. The market is global. There are Vietnamese nail salons (nail bars) in England, Japan, Australia and around the world. The wide avail-ability and afford ability of the manicure has evolved into a beauty routine for the masses and not just for the rich. Manicures and nail art are in vogue. This trend has been fueled by social media and celebrities. There is no end in sight for nail fashion trends and services.

Despite the popularity of nail salon services, the Vietnamese nail salon itself remains a mystery. What is familiar is that most Vietnamese nail technicians are slender bare-faced females. They humbly hold a customer's hands. Or they massage their feet as a part of the manicure pedicure beauty ritual. But the respirator face mask they wear is not the only veil between them and the customer. The language barrier is a veil which adds to the mystique since many manicurists speak very little English. Most customers speak very little Vietnamese. This gap and void in communica-tion can cause stereotypes and misinformation. For instance, it has been widely claimed that some Vietnamese manicurists are unlicensed. There is a possible simple explanation for this.

As a business practice many Vietnamese manicurists give them-selves American names like Julie or Betty. In fact her real name might be Mai (golden flower) or Thi (poem). They take new names that are easy for their customers to remember and pronounce. Consequently, the name offered differs from the name printed on the business license displayed on the wall. And there are more communication issues. The questions below were found on the Internet search engine Yahoo:

Why do Asian people always open nail salons?

Why do so many Asians work in nail salons?

Do you get offended when Asian people talk in the nail salon?

What are the Vietnamese girls saying at the nail salon?

So who are the Vietnamese? What did they invent? Why are they dominant? What is their contribution to beauty culture? What are the results from their efforts? This book was written to answer those questions and more. Specifically, this book also reveals nail care history, rituals and routines, nail salon concepts and opera-tions. It also includes nail salon customer comments and reviews. It concludes with the economic and cultural impact in America and abroad.

Along the way, *Nail Salons* also reveals an underlying depth of human kindness and compassion shown by many. The kindness and compassion provided a sturdy foundation. Countless unher-alded volunteers disregarded any prevailing prejudices of the time and helped the homeless and destitute immigrant newcomers. America kept its promise to help the South Vietnamese people who helped Americans during the Vietnamese War.

Therefore, refugee stories of departure from Vietnam are relevant to the start of the nail salon business. Despite their difficult and even desperate beginnings, their example and role model is re-markable and inspiring. For, it takes courage to be a refugee. The past is left behind and the future is unknown.

Chapter 1

ESCAPE

Difficult Beginnings

From ancient times, the Vietnamese people lived according to their own government rules, customs and traditions. However, France decided to rule Vietnam and did so for 60 years. During that time, in 1940 Japan invaded portions of Vietnam. This meant that Vietnam had two foreign powers within its borders. France and Japan both imposed their political influences, cultures and traditions upon the Vietnamese people. The situation was tense.

Enter Ho Chi Minh. Who was that guy?

Before he became known as Ho Chi Minh, he worked as a cook's helper and a hotel bell-boy. His journey from being a menial laborer to holding the position of President of North Vietnam took an indirect path. First, he traveled the world including America's Harlem, China, France, England and Russia. In total he lived 30 years outside of Vietnam. He then returned to his homeland as a revolutionary communist leader. Japan left. He was determined to remove the French and restore Vietnam's independence based on communist political ideas.

At that time, Vietnam consisted of North and South. Ho Chi Minh wanted to unite North Vietnam with the South under communism. South Vietnam resisted. South Vietnam's resistance was supported and helped by France and the United States. The

United States did not want communism to spread. The war was on and fighting was fierce. France stopped fighting and got out of Vietnam. The United States stayed and along with several other countries fought North Vietnam. Sixty thousand American lives were lost. The nation was somber. Jimi Hendrix played the song Star Spangled Banner at the famous Woodstock festival. It was 1969. The sorrowful tune reflected the feelings of many American people at home, especially the activist youth.

The people of South Vietnam were allies to the United States and provided many much-needed services, supplies and military manpower. Finally, North Vietnamese forces took over the capital city of South Vietnam in April 1975. The capital city once called Saigon was then re-named Ho Chi Minh City. The communists had won the war.

It was 1975. There was no longer a South Vietnam. For their loyalty to the United States, the people of South Vietnam would pay a heavy price if they remained there. To avoid capture thousands committed suicide after the North Vietnamese take over. An estimated 165,000 South Vietnamese died in "re-education camps" where slave labor was imposed. Up to 200,000 South Vietnamese were executed outright. Between 1975 and 1987 as many as 2.5 million people died of political violence. Those who lived and were able fled for their lives from South Vietnam.

Exodus by Air

It was April 27, 1975. Fourteen years of war between communist North Vietnam and South Vietnam (supported by America) was finally over. The original American military evacuation plan called for evacuation by airplane from Saigon. Saigon, the capital city was one of the departure points. As a warning that the day and time had come, an American radio station repeatedly played a specific song, "White Christmas." This was the pre-arranged signal for American personnel and friendly Vietnamese to go immediately to a designated evacuation point. It was 8:00 am. It was reported by 9:30 am that hostile North Vietnamese were moving toward the Saigon evacuation point.

The original evacuation plan called for departure by fixed wing airplane. This plan had long been drawn up and approved at the highest levels of American military personnel. That morning rock-ets and heavy artillery destroyed the airport runway. Scattered debris and continued shelling made landing and take-off impos-sible. At the last minute the emergency evacuation plan had to be changed. Helicopters would be used instead of fixed wing air-planes to airlift people onto military ships in the South China Sea.

There was a new evacuation site at a local compound. Buses moved through the city picking up passengers. By evening 395 Americans and more than 4000 Vietnamese had been evacu-ated. U.S. Marines who were providing security were beginning to withdraw. They were arranging destruction of files, and American equipment so they would not fall into the hands of the North Vietnamese.

The original evacuation plan did not include a large helicopter operation at the United States Embassy in Saigon. During the course of the evacuation, several thousand people were stranded at the embassy. Most were Vietnamese. They hoped to claim refugee status and gathered outside; some even attempted to scale embassy walls while others were repelled from mounting helicopters which were full to capacity. Desperate mothers frantically attempted to hand their infants to strangers inside the gates. Vietnamese security police did their best to maintain order with the promise that they too would be given refugee status. The sky was filled with thunder and lightning, but evacuation continued throughout the night.

On the third day, another important part of the evacuation plan was changed. At the beginning the plan provided for evacuation of Americans and Vietnamese refugees. In fact, the air evacuation from Saigon was intended as the largest transport of refugees ever attempted. It was called Operation Frequent Wind. The Pentagon had planned for the movement of 175,000 South Vietnamese. This group was in special danger of being executed by the com-munists for their service to the South Vietnam government or the United States. Some had worked as language interpreters, pilots, radio operators, office managers, equipment and food managers and in other aspects of military intelligence and security logistics.

In reality, only a small fraction of that number was evacuated. On that morning the refugee evacuation was stopped. From that point, only Americans would be evacuated. Helicopter space was tight. An American Ambassador's wife chose to leave her personal suitcase behind so a South Vietnamese woman could squeeze on board the helicopter with her. For political reasons, neither the North nor South Vietnamese intervened in the airlifts of the Americans and refugees.

THUAN LE

Thuan Le lived in Saigon. She went to college and was a teacher before marrying Trang Lai, a pilot and Lieutenant Colonel in the South Vietnamese Air Force. They had three children aged 4, 2 and 8 months old. Trang's father, Thai Lai, was ill and lived with them because he needed their help. They lived at Tan Son Nhat Air Force Base.

In 1975 the Vietnam War was at a high point. The Communists attacked many cities near Saigon. In April the fighting got too close to Saigon. The people who were related to Americans or who worked for Americans were entitled to be air-lifted out of Vietnam. The Vietnamese Air Force had a special program for pilot's wives and children to be flown to Thailand or the Philippines when the critical time came.

Thuan's husband Trang urged her to take the children and leave. Thuan didn't feel she could handle leaving her husband, father-in-law and her parents behind. So, she refused to go. Thuan tried to delay as long as possible hoping for a miracle.

On April 28th the Communists attacked the air base. Artillery and mortars poured through the base. It was worse through the night. The next morning on April 29th, artillery fire was less heavy. Trang drove his military jeep to headquarters to assess the situation. He knew by then that it was very late. He rushed home and asked his family to get into the family car. He thought the family's civilian car would be less a target than the military jeep.

He wanted to take the family to Thuan's parents' house which was outside the base. The car had been driven just the day before and worked fine. Strangely, on that day the car would not start. Trang told his family to switch to the jeep even though he knew it was a more dangerous target for snipers.

At that desperate moment an Army jeep approached driven by an Army captain. He stopped and told Trang that the deputy com-mander ordered dismissal for everybody. He told Trang to take his family to his squadron where the pilots were searching for planes to take off. Instead of taking the family off the air base, Trang quickly drove them to his friend's squadron in spite of the dam-age, noise, artillery and bombs.

When they got to the squadron, many people were there waiting in a ditch. Thuan carried the infant. Thuan's younger sister who was visiting for several days carried two of the children. Trang car-ried his ill father piggyback. Trang realized that their two year old had been placed on the wrong plane. He retrieved her. They heard later that plane was hit by a bomb.

In the midst of the chaos, the family flew away from Tan Son Nhat Air Force Base.

Thanks to their lucky encounter with the captain, they were un-harmed. Without his guidance they would have been stranded at Thuan's parents' house instead of departing from the air base.

As they flew over Saigon, Thuan looked down and saw fire and smoke rising from the blazing city. Her tears fell knowing her parents and her other siblings were left behind. She remembered that her parents had fled from the communists in North Vietnam to South Vietnam when she was a child. Now as an adult she was fleeing the communists without them. This time she was fleeing South Vietnam leaving her parents behind. She felt pain in her heart. She looked at her three children and knew she had to be strong for them.

The plane they were traveling on was in poor condition and did not have enough fuel to take them all the way to their destination. They had to land on Con Son Island off Vietnam. Con Son held a big prison full of dangerous criminals and prisoners of war. The island was crowded with thousands of others who were also fleeing Saigon. Thuan feared that the criminals and prisoners would escape.

They were frightened.

They spent the night hovering under the wing of a plane. The next morning on April 30th, they heard on the radio that Saigon had surrendered. Everyone was in tears. They had to leave Con Son as quickly as possible. There were only so many planes. Who would go and who would be left behind? It was a tense situation. With the efforts of the pilots, they found eight usable airplanes on the island. They waited and watched as others boarded. Fortunately, families were given first priority. Finally, Thuan's family had a chance to board the very last plane. It was so crowded, that her son could not catch his breath and was unable to breathe. He was resuscitated with oxygen.

They were flown to Thailand where all the men had to change from their military clothing to civilian clothes. When Thuan saw the piles of lifeless pilots' uniforms on the ground she knew in her heart that her old life was over. In Thailand they were given food and milk by the Red Cross. They then flew to Guam on an American airplane.

In Guam they were processed for refugee status and allowed to choose a country where they could resettle with relatives who already lived in France, Canada, Australia, Britain or the United States. Thuan's husband had been trained in the United States as a pilot. He hoped to work as a pilot there, although his hopes were never realized. He also had an aunt living in the United States.

They chose the United States.

They were then flown to Camp Pendleton, a Marine Corps base in San Diego County. They were among the first refugee groups to arrive in the hastily set-up tent city. The Marines were helpful in providing food and clothing, and they tried to make the refugees comfortable. Thuan's family slept on cots and shared the big tent with many other families. Every day the children cried and wanted to go home.

It was freezing, Thuan thought. She had been accustomed to 80 degree temperatures in Vietnam. When the sun went down she was afraid of the cold weather and she had no warm clothes for the children. She made coats for them from blankets. But they were safe and they were together as a family.

Camp Pendleton

Within a month Camp Pendleton became very crowded with new waves of refugees. Thuan Le's family and 80 other families signed up to take a bus north near Sacramento in Northern California. The destination in Colfax was called "Hope Village." Hope Village was not the end of Thuan's journey; it was just the beginning. At that point in time she could not know that she would become one of the first 20 Vietnamese manicurists in the United States.

Crowded Camp Pendleton

YEN RIST

Yen Rist (formerly Bach Yen Thi Nguyen) had no idea how dramati-cally her secure life would change in just a few short months. Nor did she know that her life would become intertwined with Thuan Le's life. This is her story.

Yen was a single, 27 year old secretary. She was bi-lingual having studied English as a second language in high school and at the prestigious and expensive Vietnamese-American Association. This qualified her to work in the public health department of USAID the

U.S. State Department in Saigon. She had been hearing vague radio rumors about ongoing communist activities. Still, Yen had been repeatedly reassured that there was no immediate cause for alarm. But there was a change in tone in the early weeks of April 1975. Yen began to notice that many highly placed American administrators, co-workers and their wives were suddenly and qui-etly leaving the country. Then, the head of the health department, his Vietnamese wife and their adopted son left the country. Their departure made it all too clear that the time had come to get out of Vietnam.

At that point lower ranked employees like Yen were provided pa-pers allowing them to leave Vietnam with family members. Yen's mother died when Yen was 11 years old. Yen's family at that time consisted of two brothers, a sister, her father and her grandpar-ents. There were age restrictions for departure. Siblings were required to be under the age of 18 to qualify. Her sister was 15.
One of her brothers was just 16 so he qualified. Her other brother was 20 and would have to be left behind.

Yen's father decided that he too would stay since he and the elder son could take care of themselves. He urged Yen to take the elderly grandparents with her as they would need care. The evacuation arrangements were made possible by the Indochina Migration and Refugee Assistance Act.

With papers in hand, Yen and her family proceeded to the airport. Many people were waiting there. They waited three days before being placed on a cargo plane. There were no seats on the plane. They sat on the floor, shoulder to shoulder packed in like sardines. It was April 29, 1975 just one day before the Fall of Saigon marked the end of the War in Vietnam.

They flew to the Philippines first, and then on to Guam for fur-ther processing. They stayed in Guam for three months with Yen again using her bi-lingual skills to help the Americans process in-coming refugees. Meanwhile, she was anxiously awaiting news of her older brother and father. She hoped they had found a way to escape. She would never see her father again. But her brother was found on Wake Island and reunited with the family through efforts of the Red Cross. Together again, they were flown to Camp Pendleton in California.

After several months at Camp Pendleton, The Food for the Hungry project located refugee sponsors in San Diego, Santa Ana, Texas and Sacramento California. The offer in Texas came with several acres of land. Yen's grandfather advised that she had no experi-ence with land or farming so Texas was out of consideration. Yen was undecided because she knew nothing about the history or background of the other cities.

To decide between the locations, Yen wrote the name of each city on a piece of paper. She threw the pieces into the air and picked one. "Everything is fate, and everything is as it's meant to be," she said. "We let God decide for us." She picked Sacramento, California, which would later play a pivotal role in her future.

MINH T. and KIEN T. NGUYEN

The Nguyens (Nguyen is a popular surname like Smith) met at a meditation group in Vietnam around 1969. Minh also known as Diem was a high ranking navy commander in the South Vietnamese military. Before they had their first child, Tam, Kien worked in personnel at a health facility. With the thought of more children coming, the couple decided it would be better for Kien to work from home. So Kien interned with a local beauty shop and learned hair, nail and facial care. A business license was not necessary. The couple then lived upstairs from Kien's beauty shop.

All went well until bombs started falling around them, in April, after the communists had taken Saigon. The couple had to leave and they had to leave immediately because Minh would be persecuted as a military official. In all the chaos, there was such a rush that Kien and Minh were separated. Kien was three months pregnant and ran while holding their one-year-old son. Somehow, she was placed on a plane and sent on her way out of Vietnam.

Kien thought of her parents who were being left behind. "They were old and the future was unknown." She had no choice but to leave them. Mother and child were flown to a processing camp at Fort Chaffee, Arkansas.

Meanwhile, Minh had been flown alone to Camp Pendleton, U.S.A. There the Red Cross re-united the couple. They were processed for eligibility and finally left the camp on July 12, 1975 to start a new life. By that time their daughter Linh was born in Santa Cruz, California. She was born on Thanksgiving Day. They looked to the future.

Despite their traumatic escape Thuan Le, Yen Rist and Minh and Kien Nguyen were fortunate to depart from Vietnam via air transport. Many lacked a connection to the South Vietnamese military or the United States. Others lacked the money or luck to leave by air. They were left to escape by land or sea. The situation was desperate.

Exodus by Land

Many people ran for their very lives, literally. They took with them only the clothes on their backs and as much food as they could carry. They hoped to reach any nearby country where they might stay in a refugee camp for months or even years. They ran through vast open fields and forests. After the food was gone, they ate roots, leaves, berries and an occasional field mouse or rat.

One refugee woman recounted the following scenario: "I was about 10 years old when we were crossing the river. I picked up my cousin who was 4 years old and carried her piggyback into the river. As we ran, shots rang out. My cousin cried out. She had been hit with two bullets. She was holding onto my back so tightly that when I reached the shore, her dead body had to be pried off my back."

Exodus by Sea

It was clear, the people who did not flee by air or land would face years of hard labor, death and imprisonment. Those who could do so, made desperate efforts to leave Vietnam by sea. By the end of spring the Mekong River was sprinkled with tiny boats filled with South Vietnamese soldiers and their families. They hoped to survive the long 600-mile journey to the shores of Malaysia. The exodus of the Vietnamese had only just begun.

Boat people

Kim

Kim was a refugee who shared this story. She fled along with her husband and children on a small boat for the 21-day journey. The boat was barely seaworthy and was crowded. Eight days passed on the turbulent sea. People were ill and fainting for lack of food. Their boat was seized by armed Thai pirates who fed them, then robbed them of their few possessions. Kim's baby began to cry. One man threw Kim's infant into the sea. Fortunately, they were able to retrieve the baby. A young girl on board was kidnapped by the men and later sold into slavery or prostitution. Kim had purposefully worn men's clothes, cut her hair short and greased her face to appear unattractive. The men did not molest her.

Kim's boat was a "little fish." The "little fish" was intended to meet up further out at sea with a "big fish" which would take them out of Vietnam's territorial waters. They made it to a "big fish." The boat, a fishing vessel, was about 25 feet long. It was important that the boat appear to be only a fishing boat, so all 120 refugees had to stay hidden, below deck, for safety's sake. It was very crowded. People did not have room to stand. They had to remain in a fetal position. They stayed that way for three days.

After leaving Vietnam's maritime border, passengers were permit-ted outside the hold to get fresh air. Even that was frightening since the waves were high, and most passengers had never been to sea before.

To make matters worse, there was no food or water. A "little fish" loaded with food was supposed to meet them, but due to a com-munications error, the meeting did not occur. From time to time they would get lucky. A passing "big fish" would throw food and water to them. Finally, they made it to Malaysia only to find that Malaysia was not accepting any more Vietnamese boat people.

The Royal Malaysian Navy did, however, give them a bigger boat, food and water. The boat people were instructed to go to an island in Indonesia where they were picked up and given rice and food. Afterward, they were taken to a refugee camp at Galang. Kim's story is not uncommon.

Later, Vietnam expelled 745,000 ethnic Chinese from the country. They were placed on crowded boats and put out to sea. They com-prised the bulk of the large second wave of refugees that began leaving Vietnam in late 1978. They too were the "boat people." An international crisis had begun. Thousands upon thousands drowned.

A dire fate awaited the residents who stayed in South Vietnam. Friends of the Americans, shopkeepers, government workers and intellectuals were kicked out of Vietnam's cities. They were redirected to "new economic zones," remote areas which the new Vietnamese government wanted to become fruitful. There they were forced to do agricultural work. During the day they performed hard and dangerous work. During the evenings they were required to attend political classes designed to re-educate them to conform to communist society.

Many individuals were sentenced to consecutive terms after completing original sentences of three or five years. This was the fate also of those who were caught trying to flee the country. The death and suicide rates were very high in the Vietnamese labor camps. Camp conditions offered very little food and no medicine. Human Rights Committee President singer Joan Baez protested along with others in the international community.

Chapter 2

OPERATION NEW LIFE

The United States, Canada, France, Britain and Australia were among the countries which took in Indochinese refugees. Vietnamese refugees able to leave via land air or sea were initially settled in the United States at four points of entry. Camps for processing the refugees were located in California, Florida, Pennsylvania and Arkansas. The function of the camp was to interview each refugee to determine eligibility, admissibility and their desired country of settlement. In the camp scattered fam-ily members were re-united, and orphans were identified includ-ing Amer-Asian children of Vietnamese and American soldiers. Personal identification materials and needed medical attention were also provided.

Thousands of Asian Vietnamese, Hmong, Laotian and Cambodians inhabited the camps on a temporary basis. All of them were in danger of retaliation from the North Vietnamese government for helping America's military effort. Most inhabitants were political refugees and were granted permanent, legal residence in the United States. While they differed in language, customs, values, religion and traditions, they had in common an opportunity for a new life. One Indochina Resettlement Program was aptly called "Operation New Life."

Resettlement programs like "Operation New Life" were funded under The 1975 Indochina Migration and Refugee Assistance

Act. After evacuations, the purpose and aim of the act was to find refugees safe residences in the United States. It represented the promise made and kept by the American government to help those who had helped America. Many governmental and chari-table groups worked to find volunteer sponsors and host families for newly processed refugees so they could be relocated from the camps.

After entering the processing camps, refugees were then quickly rotated out and placed in cities around the United States. Once a locale was provided, refugees qualified for state welfare and so-cial service benefits. Cash and medical assistance was provided for up to three years. Services in language training, education and job assistance were also provided to help refugees become integrated into a state's social and economic community. The re-location programs cost millions of dollars at a time when national unemployment was high.

The response of average Americans to the influx of the refugees was as mixed as the general public's political response to the Vietnam War. For some the response was charitable and humani-tarian as many American families hosted and provided support to the refugees. For others, the response was hostile for they chose to make no distinction between the North and South Vietnamese. Refugees were simply Vietnamese, the people who had killed 60 thousand American soldiers. Other responses were purely racist.

THUAN LE

After a crowded and stressful time at Camp Pendleton, Thuan and her family arrived at Hope Village near Sacramento, California.

They were relieved to find that they would stay in an old building which was formerly a hospital. They were assigned rooms with a bath and shower. Finally, they had some privacy and a roof over their heads. The refugees took turns helping with cooking and cleaning. Thuan appreciated the beautiful isolated location which was far from the city. It was heavily wooded with pine trees and abundant with deer. The setting allowed her nerves to calm down to some extent although she still worried about her country, her parents and siblings left behind in Vietnam.

Soon she began to hear talk of actress Tippi Hedren, an acquaintance of Vietnamese actress Kieu Chinh, visiting the refugees at Hope Village. Those refugees were an elite group among the first wave of refugees to leave Vietnam. Many were former military officials and their educated wives. Some spoke or understood spoken English. Tippi brought her famous movie *The Birds* and showed it to the women so they would understand her profession. Word spread that Tippi Hedren was a beautiful lady who cared about them. She was a volunteer member of the Food for the Hungry organization. She started meeting with the women. At first, Thuan was unable to attend the meetings because of child care duties.

Thuan Le with her three children

When she was able to attend a meeting, Tippi told the women they would need a career when they left Hope Village.

Thuan then learned that a sewing class and a typing class were being offered. Thuan knew how to sew, but she was not familiar with American patterns. Thuan didn't like typing and missed a few classes. Tippi visited the women again and looked at them "with a worried eye."

At that meeting, Thuan, and the women were amazed at Tippi's long, red manicured fingernails. Tippi's eyes lit up and a big smile came across her face. Tippi then announced that they would have a manicure class. Thuan thought to herself that nobody in Vietnam showed interest in learning to manicure nails. She discussed it with her husband, Trang. They were both very skeptical about manicuring as a potential career. But Tippi insisted saying "Oh no, don't underestimate manicuring. Movie stars and the movie industry need manicurists. It would be very glamorous. You could be flown to a movie location just to fix a nail! We will train you to be very special manicurists," Tippi said. Tippi had to convince and persuade them. Thuan and the women finally yielded to her charismatic influence.

Every weekend Tippi visited and brought her personal manicurist, Dusty Coots, to teach the women. Tippi gave each of the women a manicure set. "She encouraged us with love and smiles." The women eagerly awaited her visit every weekend. Thuan said, "When Tippi arrived they ran to her just as children do when their mother comes home." After all Tippi was oldest and she was a great mentor.

They responded by working hard to learn manicuring. Tippi even recommended that in addition to the basic manicure they should learn how to perform "*Juliette* nail wrap" an advanced technique.

Manicurists charge more for that procedure. They practiced on Tippi. During the week they practiced techniques on each other. They also practiced speaking English because Tippi advised that English would be needed in their careers. Thuan had studied English in high school and did at least understand spoken English. But, it was still a challenge for her.

YEN RIST

Yen had chosen Sacramento as her family's destination, and they were on their way to Hope Village in California. They waited well over an hour upstairs at the Sacramento Airport until they were paged. Soon some Vietnamese men and a "beautiful lady" ap-proached them as they were the only family that appeared to be waiting. The beautiful lady was actress Tippi Hedren. She told the family that she had been waiting for them downstairs! Yen recalls that in her youth she had seen the movie *The Birds* and remembered the beautiful actress. "I never dreamed that I would meet her."

Tippi informed Yen that she was in the process of enrolling women in a manicuring class at the Citrus Heights Beauty College. They stopped by the college and Yen was eager to enroll. She remem-bers the people there were "very kind." The family was then trans-ported to Hope Village in Sacramento and installed in lodging at the former hospital. Soon Yen joined Thuan Le and 18 others for the daily ride to the beauty college.

The old station wagon

BECKY AND CHARLES HAMBELTON

Becky and Charles Hambelton founded the Citrus Heights Beauty College in 1969 at Citrus Heights, California. One day in 1975 glamorous actress Tippi Hedren came into the college and implored them to consider enrolling 20 Vietnamese refugee women in their 400-hour manicure course. The Hambeltons decided to accept them. They were aware that only a few of the women could speak English but the Hambeltons felt those few would prove to be helpful to the others.

The Hambeltons were able to enroll the students without charging tuition because of an existing relationship with the local school district to provide vocational training. When asked why they did it, Becky said, "They left their home country with nothing, they needed to have a chance and if they were willing to make sacri-fices, then we would sacrifice also. Because we had a better life, they would also."

The women did sacrifice. The college was 45 minutes from Hope Village, where two old station wagons were parked. Senior citizen volunteers and husbands of the women drove them to and from school daily. Thuan and the others brought their lunches and stayed at the school all day. When they returned home after dinner they studied together. They had to learn the anatomy of the hand and master the terminology they would face on the written exam. The exam was in English. They struggled.

Citrus Heights Beauty College 1975

Help and assistance came from unlikely resources.

For instance, during the day, one of the Vietnamese women would translate Becky's instructions in English into Vietnamese for the rest of the women. The woman also translated the English textbooks into Vietnamese. In another example, the college had a dress code. All students were required to wear white uniforms and white shoes. The women had none. Volunteers scoured thrift shops, found used uniforms and donated them to the women.

In yet another example, the salon management portion of the training course required the women to practice answering telephones. A local phone company provided two phones without charge to the college so the women could practice. It also helped that the college often didn't charge customers so appointments would be available for every student to gain practice time. Customers then in turn came frequently and specifically requested the services of the Vietnamese women. This was a morale boost for them.

"We were all amazed. The women completed the 400-hour course in just 10 weeks with help from many caring people, Becky said." The college administration and the other students held a gradua-tion party to honor the women. Everyone was impressed with how hard the women worked.

The 20 Vietnamese students: Tippi Hedren and a volunteer, top center. A fellow student bottom left. Becky and Charles Hambelton, far right.

Congratulatory signatures from classmates

To show their appreciation, the women prepared a Vietnamese style lunch for the other students. They gave Becky and Tippi Vietnamese-style dresses. A second celebration cake was shared.

The grateful students hosted a Vietnamese-style
lunch at the beauty college. Tippi Hedren and a
volunteer attended.

A second graduation cake was shared. Becky Hambelton,
top center.

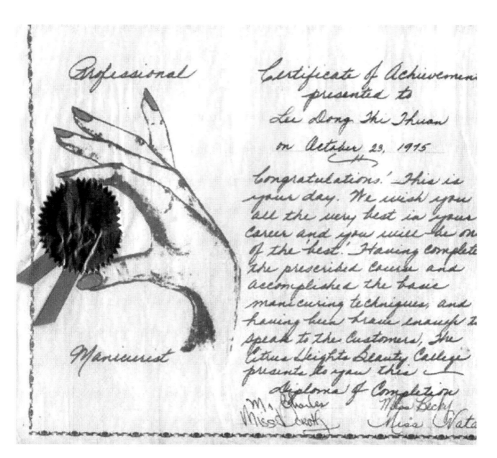

Thuan Le's Certificate of Achievement signed by Becky
Hambleton known as Miss Becky and Charles known as Mr.
Charles Hambelton, owners of Citrus Heights Beauty College.

With Beauty college graduation now over, it was time to face the California State Manicure License Examination. Each student was allowed to have someone help them during the written state exam. Trang, Thuan's husband, had learned the terminology so he could assist her during the exam.

It was quite a production. All 20 of the women would take both the written licensing exam and the practice exam on the same day. To accomplish this, many fellow college students volunteered as live models for the practice portion of the exam. In this way all of the women could take the practice exam following the written exam. All went well.

Winter came and they still did not know whether they had passed the exams. Tippi came to see them and told them they had all passed the written and practice tests. They were relieved and happy and celebrated. Tippi gave Thuan and each woman a letter of introduction and referral to show prospective employers.

She also told them to stay in touch!

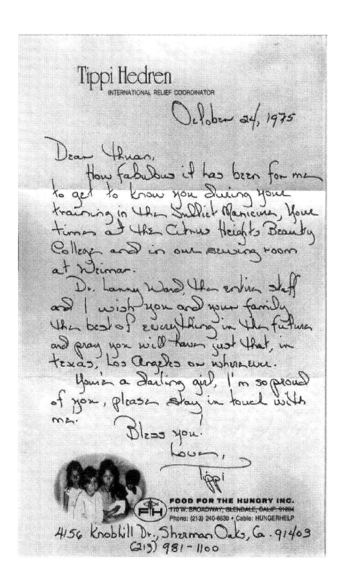

Tippi Hedren
INTERNATIONAL RELIEF COORDINATOR

October 24, 1975

Dear Thuan,

How fabulous it has been for me to get to know you during your training in the Sullict Manicure, your times at the Citrus Heights Beauty College and in our sewing room at Weimar.

Dr. Lanny Ward, the entire staff and I wish you and your family the best of everything in the future and pray you will have just that, in Texas, Los Angeles or wherever.

You're a darling girl, I'm so proud of you, please stay in touch with me.

Bless you.

Love,

Tippi

FOOD FOR THE HUNGRY INC.
110 W. BROADWAY, GLENDALE, CALIF. 91004
Phone: (213) 240-6630 • Cable: HUNGERHELP

4156 Knobhill Dr., Sherman Oaks, Ca. 91403
(213) 981-1100

Tippi congratulates Thuan Le for completing manicure
training.

Refugees board the bus for a long trip to Los Angeles and a new life.

Hope Village closes. Sacramento Bee Newspaper November 2, 1975. In the article, Trang Lai mentions that his wife Thuan Le's completion of manicure training would be helpful to the family in the future.

Shortly thereafter, the time at Hope Village ended as families received sponsors and left for other cities. One of the future mani-curists observed that in Vietnam she was rich and had a manicur-ist; now she would *be* a manicurist herself!

THUAN LE

Thuan and her family were sponsored by a church in Santa Monica, California called St. Augustine by the Sea. The church rented a two bedroom apartment and filled it with used furniture donated by church members. Thuan's family was grateful. After a few months they wanted to be independent from the church, so the church would be free to sponsor other families. With help from the church, Thuan's family vacated the apartment for other refugee families to use.

Thuan had her manicure license and a letter of introduction, but, she didn't know what to do next.

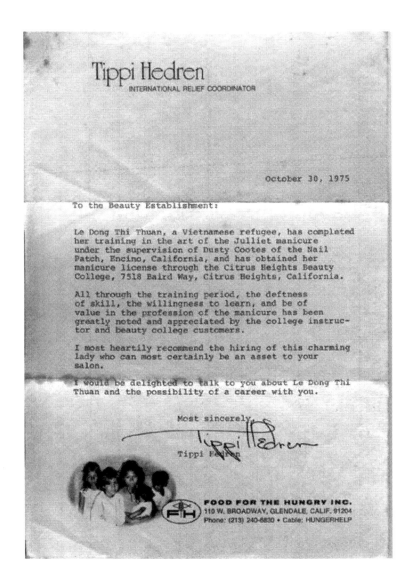

Tippi Hedren
INTERNATIONAL RELIEF COORDINATOR

October 30, 1975

To the Beauty Establishment:

Le Dong Thi Thuan, a Vietnamese refugee, has completed
her training in the art of the Julliet manicure
under the supervision of Dusty Cootes of the Nail
Patch, Encino, California, and has obtained her
manicure license through the Citrus Heights Beauty
College, 7518 Baird Way, Citrus Heights, California.

All through the training period, the deftness
of skill, the willingness to learn, and be of
value in the profession of the manicure has been
greatly noted and appreciated by the college instructor and beauty college customers.

I most heartily recommend the hiring of this charming
lady who can most certainly be an asset to your
salon.

I would be delighted to talk to you about Le Dong Thi
Thuan and the possibility of a career with you.

Most sincerely,

Tippi Hedren

FOOD FOR THE HUNGRY INC.
110 W. BROADWAY, GLENDALE, CALIF. 91204
Phone: (213) 240-6830 • Cable: HUNGERHELP

Tippi's letter of recommendation for Thuan Le

So she called Tippi!

Tippi Hedren
INTERNATIONAL RELIEF COORDINATOR

October 31, 1975

Dear Thuan:

Congratulations on passing the California State Board of Cosmetology for your manicure license! I'm so very proud of you. You have really done something that you, too, should be very proud of.

Now, you have your license, and the reference letter. Please take both with you on all interviews. Remember, look your prettiest, and be as talkative as you possibly can. You have had the best training, so feel secure that you can handle the job!

When you need to buy manicure supplies, find a beauty supply shop where you can get your needs at a discount. Do not buy at a drug store or department store, it is too expensive that way.

Remember, TIME IS MONEY, and the faster you can do a perfect manicure, the more customers you can do in a day and the happier your customer will be. This is most important with the Julliet! I can't stress enough how necessary it is to get the times down to one hour, (for both hands) like I've been telling you all along. I know you can do it, you've proven that you're very capable already.

Now, good luck on your interviews! God bless you.

Love,

Tippi

Tippi Hedren

P.S. Write to me!

FOOD FOR THE HUNGRY INC.
110 W. BROADWAY, GLENDALE, CALIF. 91204
Phone: (213) 240-6830 • Cable: HUNGERHELP

Tippi encouraged Thuan Le

Within days, Tippi came to Thuan's apartment to meet with her. At the kitchen table, Tippi extended her hand to Thuan and asked for a manicure even though her manicure had been freshly done and looked pretty. Tippi wanted to see for herself just how good Thuan was at her new skill. The children were running and screaming around the apartment. They were carrying pillow cases stuffed with belongings and pretending they were running away from war. This made Thuan even more nervous as she completed the mani-cure. It took one hour. Tippi was patient throughout that time and was very happy with the results.

A few days later Tippi returned and took Thuan out to a relaxing lunch to calm her down. Then, she took Thuan to an upscale beau-ty shop in the area and introduced her to the owner. The owner hired Thuan although four American manicurists were already employed there. It was her first paid manicure job.

Thuan was the only Vietnamese in the shop. She was new and spent a lot of time sitting and waiting. The other manicurists had established customers and were kept busy. Eventually, customers learned about her unique nail wrap specialty and asked for her services. The shop was open seven days a week. Thuan worked part-time on the three days that nobody else wanted, Sunday, Monday and Tuesday. She was also somewhat disappointed that her customers were elderly women who did not want a fancy manicure or nail polish; they wanted a basic manicure or a nail trim, the cheapest service of all. Of course that meant that the tip would also be small.

Thuan Le at her first manicure job.

When a customer asked for a pedicure Thuan hoped the owner would put her in the back corner of the shop so people wouldn't see her doing a pedicure. She was also embarrassed to tell her friends that she "did" nails. She got over that. Thuan kept that job despite the fact that she had to take two buses to get to the beauty salon. She added manicure jobs at other shops until she built up a clientèle at the first job. At that time there were not any Asian nail shops. Clients were difficult to attract outside of locations in upscale areas. Thuan persevered. After a few years Thuan built up a clientèle.

YEN RIST

When their time at Hope Village came to an end, Yen's family and others were sponsored by organizations and dispersed to several cities. Yen took her sister, 2 brothers and grandparents along with the majority leaving for Los Angeles.

Once there, Tippi found a job for Yen as a manicurist at a Beverly Hills salon. It didn't work out. The customers there wanted to stay with their current manicurist. They didn't want to try a newcomer. So, Yen had no customers to provide income. Yet parking cost $8.00 per day. Yen could not afford the location. She told Tippi she needed another job. "Tippi she took her time and she did so much to help us. She did everything to help us. She was a true friend," Yen said.

Tippi found another job for Yen in Orange County. At about that time acrylic nails were becoming popular, so Tippi enrolled Yen in a class in Costa Mesa to learn the new technique. It was a one-week course which otherwise would have cost $2000 per person. Tippi arranged for the course to be free of charge for Yen. Yen became the first Vietnamese manicurist to learn and practice the acrylic nail extension technique and application.

Yen went on to practice as a manicurist for a few years. Seeking higher pay and better working conditions, she moved from Orange County back to Beverly Hills and then back to Orange County. Palm Springs followed, then L.A., Beverly Hills and back to Palm Springs.

Yen was a hard worker. She worked two jobs doing nails and hair styling. She had siblings and grandparents to support. She needed money. "Every dollar I make helps a lot of people," she says in reference to financial support she provides for her family including relatives in Vietnam. "Anytime my customers want my service, I am there. I never say 'no'."

MINH AND KIEN NGUYEN

When their refugee camp days were over, Kien relied on her experience as a beauty shop owner in Vietnam. She got a job working in a beauty salon. She worked for 10 years, saving for the day they would have their own business. Meanwhile, her husband Minh Nguyen was working as a social worker at a government agency helping refugees. He knew first hand that the refugees were desperate for jobs and income to survive in American society.

In California, they were surprised when reading the Vietnamese language newspaper to see an article about Thuan Le. Thuan Le and Kien had gone to high school together in Vietnam. The article mentioned that Thuan Le was a manicurist and gave the address of the salon where she was working. Kien and Minh went there to surprise her. They went away very impressed with the posh surroundings in which Thuan was working with only a manicuring license. They liked the idea of manicuring as a career because it required a relatively small amount of training and English language skill. Minh was confidant in recommending manicuring as a career to his clients.

While working at the government agency, Minh put Kien through beauty college, where she earned a cosmetology license. He saw that she had customers and was doing very well, and he wanted to open a beauty salon for her. It was his idea but Kien was scared. She was a reluctant entrepreneur. She wanted the security of being able to pay their bills from her established job. She gave in. Minh himself then went to beauty college and joined her at their business, Tam Beauty Salon in West Covina, California. It was 1977.

By 1980 they opened another business, Personality Beauty Salon in Pasadena, California. Both salons were full-service salons pro-viding hair, nail and facial care. They worked hard.

Eight years later they sold both salons and opened the first Vietnamese beauty college, Advance Beauty College in Garden Grove, California. According to Kien, Minh ran everything in the college. He was janitor, cleaner, manager and sometimes manicurist. "Sometimes he even slept in the office at night!" But, hard work paid off.

Minh laid the foundation for the college's success by first traveling to Vietnamese communities from state to state sharing his knowledge and belief that manicuring was a great vocation and career. He and Kien could provide training. Still there remained a serious obstacle. The obstacle was the written state licensing examination which was in English.

The obstacle was removed. Minh, Kien and another couple later successfully advocated and lobbied for cosmetology licensing exams written in the Vietnamese language. They explained to the officials that many people had experience and good skills, but the test in English was very hard for them. The officials relented. State manicure license exams were translated into the Vietnamese lan-guage. This was the pole that vaulted immigrant manicurists over the high hurdle. This was a tremendous benefit to the Vietnamese non-English speaking community.

Chapter 3

MANICURE HISTORY

The Vietnamese, of course, did not invent nail care. Excavators of royal tombs at Babylonia from 3200 B.C. found the first manicure set. It was made of pure gold! It was likely used on men who wore nail paste made from henna or Kohl. The color of the nail paste represented the station or class of the male. Black was worn by the highest classes while green was worn by lower classes. From the 1970s until today, black nail polish has regained popularity with both males and females who are following the Grunge, Goth, Rock Star and Punk trends.

Around 3000 B.C., the early Chinese also used nail color to distinguish dynasty. To create a desired color pigment, they soaked their nails for hours in a brew of beeswax, Arabic gum, flower pet-als and egg whites. This elaborate process was only for the upper classes whose choice of color reflected the colors of the ruling dynasty of the time.

In contrast, Egyptian people of all classes were allowed to use nail color. Ancient Egyptian women stained their nails with henna. However, color was still used to distinguish between classes. Lower classes of ordinary people wore pale colors while the upper classes of royalty wore shades of red. Cleopatra was said to have worn blood red color on her nails.

From Nail Paste to Nail Polish

The nail polish colors worn by ancient people were far more flamboyant than the colors worn by Europeans and Americans up until the 1800s. During the 1800s British Victorian era manicures were very simple. The nails were merely buffed, then tinted with red oil. By the 1920s a female French makeup artist, Michelle Menard began using a glossy lacquer inspired by high-gloss car paint. It was similar to the polish used today. The company which perfected the formula used pigments instead of dyes. That com-pany later became known as Revlon.

Revlon sold polish in a variety of colors at drug stores and de-partment stores. The rage for nail color in America was fueled in the 1940s by glamorous actresses who appeared in Technicolor movies. Hollywood royalty wore red nails which again symbolized the regal and elegant. The last obstacle to nail polish acceptance by the masses disappeared in 1928 when Cutex Brands, Inc. de-veloped a nail polish remover from acetone which was suitable for home use.

By the 1970s many American women preferred the more subtle French manicure designed to resemble natural nails. The tips of the nails were painted white while the base of the nails were polished in pink or a suitable nude shade. It was considered more practical and versatile and was quickly adapted after its debut in Paris when worn by models on haute couture fashion runways.

Before professional manicures were widely available, as far back as the 1930s, American working-class and rural women bought nail polish at local drugstores and did their own nails. Classic movies and film clearly depicted actors with well-groomed hands including nail polish. The lighter pink nail color polishes were pre-ferred. In real life the color red was reserved for women of a certain reputation. To avoid possible scorn, many women even removed their nail polish before attending Sunday church services. Upper class women, those married to wealthy men, and those who did not work for a living always sported manicured nails which were definitely a status symbol.

The Acrylic Nail-The Full-Set

The Vietnamese did not invent artificial nails. The modern acrylic nail was invented and patented by a dentist named Fred Slack in the 80s, who had broken a nail. Acrylic nails are known as artificial nails, nail extensions, nail enhancements or fake nails. Artificial nails are created in a number of ways. Nail extensions made from acrylic can be created using tips or forms. Tips are glued to the end of the nails and acrylic is spread over the entire nail. Forms, however, are fitted over the nail while acrylic is used to mold an artificial nail. The acrylic product used may be either liquid or powder. Another method uses "UV" Top Coat a polymer resin that is hardened under ultraviolet light.

In the modern film *Finger of Doom*, the Kung Fu fighting heroine, actress Ivy Ling Po wore long, metal nail extensions. As far back as the Ming Dynasty of China, women wore very long artificial nails or finger extensions as a symbol of elite status. Some extensions were even made of silver metal encrusted with gems. At a glance an onlooker must conclude that the woman does no manual labor or domestic work. Most American women have had experiences with acrylic nails for perhaps the same reason.

As a successful actress Tippi Hedren could afford to hire a personal manicurist. Most American working women like clerks, cashiers, receptionists, nurses, teachers, domestics or factory workers could not afford a professional manicure. A professional manicure cost about $60 at non-Vietnamese establishments in the 1970s. For this reason a manicure was perceived as a luxury service reserved for the wealthy and pampered. Average working women performed basic manicures and pedicures on themselves.

Women have always sought beauty. The manicure had already been invented. Nail polish had been invented. Nail polish remover had been invented. Nail extensions had been invented. There was a Vietnamese beauty college graduating trained manicurists. There were many trained and eager Vietnamese manicurists. These underpinnings set the stage for nail care for the masses. *Affordable* nail care for the masses was a niche just waiting to be discovered. Soon working-class clientèle would embrace nail art and acrylic nails, lengthy fake talons, and mini hand and mini leg massages. Affordable prices helped to wake up the sleepy nail care business.

The nail salon business requires licenses. Cosmetology exams were once in English only. Very soon cosmetology exams were translated into the Vietnamese language. Cosmetology instructors spoke English and Vietnamese at Vietnamese beauty colleges which quickly grew in number.

Waves of Vietnamese manicurists soon followed. They were mostly refugees, at first, who settled for low wages and lowered prices. Now, manicures and pedicures go for as little as $15 in some cities. The Cambodian people are associated with dough-nut shops, Koreans with dry cleaners, Ethiopians with parking lots and East Indians with hotels/motels or eyebrow threading. African-Americans are associated with Jazz and Hip Hop music. There are also Swedish masseuses, French hairdressers and Russian facialists. The Vietnamese are now indelibly associated with nail salon businesses.

For Vietnamese immigrants, nail care represented a way in which they could acquire a skill and make money immediately without learning to speak much English. It was a way they could overcome their language barrier in a foreign county. There were other at-tractions. As an entrepreneur they could work for themselves and eventually, for some, own a business which required very little capital outlay. For most American women nail care represented a new affordable and pleasurable beauty routine. The nail salon business was born. The word was out and the path made clear. Becoming a manicurist was one way to achieve independence in a foreign land.

Attitudes toward Manicurists

Handling the hands and feet of others may lead to independence. Independence is one thing but prestige is another. Whether they were black, white or Vietnamese, as manicurists their skills were considered low-level without prestige, and they were looked down upon. During the early days there were black-owned beauty par-lors and white-only owned beauty parlors. Black women worked in both. In full-service white-owned beauty parlors, they were al-lowed to provide shampoo or manicure services only.

Many felt that was a better job than working as a domestic cook-ing, washing and cleaning for someone else's family for $1.00 a week. Nor was it the dream job to work as an agent for black female millionaire entrepreneur Madam C. J. Walker selling hair care products to other black women. The job could earn poten-tially $100.00 per week in 1910. Still African-American women were not quick to admit that they "did" feet for a living.

Black beauticians offered or performed manicures at their own shops. It is less well-known that black women also provided manicuring services at black-owned barbershops. Bessie Coleman a lone manicurist provided manicures for wealthy African American men at Duncan's Barbershop which was located on Chicago's Stroll on the Black Wall Street in the 1920s. It was called "Black Wall Street" because many black owned businesses were located in the area.

About that same time, Tulsa, Oklahoma's Black Wall Street had Carter's barbershop on Greenwood Ave alongside a hotel, cigar store, grocery store and pool hall. Jackson Ward is a National Historic Landmark Black Wall Street area in Richmond Virginia. The famous Parrish Street in Durham, North Carolina has a public plaque, to this day, denoting Black Wall Street. Eight barbershops were there among the thriving African American businesses through the 1930s. No doubt all of the black barbershops had at least one attractive female manicurist.

Popular culture television and film perpetuated a demeaning atti-tude toward manicurists. A 1962 episode of the Andy Griffith show was titled "The Manicurist." In the episode an attractive female pretended she had knowledge of the trade at Floyd's Barbershop in order to get the attention of the town's men, but instead she ex-perienced the wrath of the town's women. This attitude was again scripted into the 1988 sci-fi comedy film *Earth Girls Are Easy*. In it actress Geena Davis played a manicurist whose spoken line was "I'm just a manicurist. I don't know anything about anything except nails."

In fact, up until the late 1970s, the United States Bureau of Labor Statistics completely ignored manicuring as a profession. Other occupations such as auto repair were listed in the North American Industry Classification System (NAICS). Manicurists had no assigned trade number. The Bureau did not keep statistics or even track growth of the occupation. That situation has changed. Manicure service is now # 812113. The personal services SIC industry code for manicure-pedicure is #7231. The U. S. Census Bureau also tracks the industry.

Still there is a significant discrepancy in official figures and nail industry statistics concerning the size of the nail industry. Federal agencies count only jobs; they do not count the self-employment status of booth renters. Owners of very small nail businesses are also not counted. These types of ownership do not fit the definition of a "small business" in terms of the Small Business Administration.

However, both official and industry statistics agree that there has been significant growth in the nail care business. By the end of the twentieth century, the nail industry was hailed as one of the fastest growing industries in the United States. It would have been difficult for early nail workers to predict the pride and self-esteem of manicurists, who later enjoyed self-employment with their own businesses. Many manicurists, also called nail technician or nail techs, provide specialized functions and also enjoy self-employment. They simply act as independent contractors by renting a booth or space in a salon owned by someone else.

Chapter 4

VIETNAMESE NAIL SALONS

What did the Vietnamese Invent?

The Vietnamese in America did not invent the manicure, nail pol-ish or artificial nails. What the Vietnamese did invent is the limited service, stand-alone nails-only establishment. The nail salon con-cept and business model separated manicuring from other beauty service venues. It was no longer necessary to go to a beauty shop for a manicure. At the outset, manicurists did not shampoo and style hair, provide facials, make-up, or shaving.

Those additional services were to be found at full-service beauty shops (parlors). Those services were provided by licensed cos-metologists. Vietnamese nail salons have been called "discount salons" because their service prices, initially were 30-50% lower than in the non-Vietnamese sector. It is not clear who coined the term. It is unlikely that the term was coined by the Vietnamese.

Minh and Kien Nguyen opened the first Vietnamese beauty salon and the first Vietnamese beauty college. Interestingly, it is not known who opened the first Vietnamese nail salon in America! It appears that the nail salon merely evolved from several necessi-ties. A manicure license was cheap and required less training. It required only a small rental space or could be located in a home. A salon required very few expensive pieces of equipment and few supplies so a salon business could be opened for a relatively small amount of money. It was a perfect situation for entrepreneurship, independence with very little English required.

More than a price difference

Vietnamese nail salons are common sights quickly spreading from inner-cities to the suburbs. Many are open from 9:00 am until 9:00 pm seven days a week. The vast majority 94% are run by Vietnamese women. In the early days, the average salons were usually small store fronts with simple names like "Happy Nail" or "Nail Pretty." Most were sparsely furnished with at least two manicure workstations. A workstation consists of a narrow table with chairs on both sides. The customer sits on one side of the table and the manicurist sits on the other side. There is a sink where customers wash their hands as a part of the procedure. A manicure takes 30-40 minutes by appointment. More time is needed if the customer is a *walk-in* who must wait for service.

The room perhaps has at least two pedicure spa massage chairs. There are a few salons in major cities now with up to 100 chairs. Chairs are the most expensive equipment in the room. A pedicure massage chair may cost up to $1,200 depending on design and manufacturer. The chairs consist of a metal frame backrest and seat covered in vinyl or leather with an attached heated fiberglass tub. The pedicurist sits on a small stool at the foot of the machine and rarely looks up. A pedicure takes 35 minutes. This secular beauty procedure bears no resemblance to the towel and bowl servitude routine of foot washing which has spiritual significance in some religions. In such routines only men are allowed to have their feet washed by another person.

Since many nail techs speak limited English, there is very little conversation during the Mani-Pedi. Conversation takes the form of a one word question like, "Color?" "Round?" "Short?" The lack of conversation helps to speed up the work of the nail tech who focuses on looking down at the nails to achieve accuracy. A customer may not desire conversation but may prefer a peaceful environment instead. As the customer's feet soak in hot water, they may choose to relax on the throne-like pedicure chair. They may use various vibratory modes on the chair while reading a magazine, listening to music or watching TV.

The time spent at a salon is a welcome break from responsibilities associated with husbands, children and jobs. A (2010) United Nations study revealed what most women already knew. That is, women world-wide work, whether paid or not, more hours than do men. A woman deserves time to herself to replenish her strength and reserves.

As a customer looks about the room, they are likely to see shelves well stocked with bowls and bottles, brushes, cotton balls and sponges with disinfectants. There are also plenty of sterilizers, sanitizers, loofahs, gloves and protective supplies; scissors, extractors and tweezers. Brightly colored bottles of nail polish decorate the room along with a few artificial flowers. There are no family pictures displayed. A small Buddhist altar usually stands unnoticed by most customers.

The nail salon has one door marked Restroom. Another door is marked Employee. The door marked Employee usually contains a small refrigerator and microwave oven to heat lunch or dinner. There may be a small bed, chair or blankets to use for resting between customers. Sometimes, a friend, husband, child or relative may be there quietly waiting. The distinctive earthy aroma of Vietnamese Fish Sauce permeates the room and often wafts into the outer room to mingle with the smell of the strong chemicals used in the manicure-pedicure process. Often, the front door is kept open. Walk-ins are welcome.

Differences in Vietnamese nail salons

The Vietnamese nail salon does not resemble the beauty parlors of yesterday. Beauty parlors were different. In contrast, loyal patrons maintained long-standing relationships with full service shops where their "beauty work" including nails, hair and make-up was done. The shop owner knew her clientèle and most had regular weekly or bi-weekly appointments. Many of her customers knew each other personally allowing for sharing of local news and community gossip. Those were neighborhood beauty parlors.

Vietnamese nail salons differ in that a customer may or may not have an appointment. The customer will generally not know any of the other customers there who are a mix of races and lifestyles. There will be no Vietnamese customers there. The salon owner or nail tech may not know the customer. It is an impersonal business exchange with an almond-eyed person often wearing a respirator face mask. The mask protects the manicurist from the acrylic dust which comes from the electric sanders which are used instead of manual buffers. Impersonal. Perhaps. Yet the experience is an intimate exchange because the manicurist holds both the hands and the feet of the customer.

How did the Vietnamese open nail salon businesses?

In the early days, nail salons were not funded by bank loans or the Small Business Administration. Instead, money came from savings accumulated and shared by family members who worked other jobs that required no English like washing cars or cleaning office buildings at night. Start-up funding may also have come from "Hui". It is an ancient Vietnamese practice similar to Chinese mutual aid societies, where money is shared within a group by agreement. Credit and investment opportunities are provided this way as an alternative to banks, the Small Business Administration or loan sharks.

There were other start-up methods. Funds to start nail salons also came later from Vietnamese workers who were laid off from pro-fessional jobs during the economic downturn in the early 1980s. Many retrained in manicuring and opened salons rather than hop-ing to return to former employers.

This often means that sons, husbands, daughters, cousins and uncles plus relatives through marriage all work together with an emotional and financial interest in building the family business. As a simple matter of economy, when more members of a family work together, more income stays in the family. Owning a busi-ness - entrepreneurship is the shared vision and goal of the family. Vietnamese culture is very family centered. It's a family affair.

It is noteworthy that women own and operate most Vietnamese nail salons. A woman may own more than one salon, sometimes with different names for each one. One woman owns 52 nail sa-lons. Unlike salons like Gene Juarez, Vietnamese generally do not use their personal names on their establishments. Names like, "Pretty Nails" instead reflect the function of the business. The nail salon as a family business may stem from Buddhist collectivist philosophy that the needs of the family come before the needs of the individual in the family. When a nail salon is opened, the entire family joins in to achieve its success. Vietnamese men now work as manicurists as well, many of them in salons owned by their wives.

TU

Tu's husband was killed fighting during the takeover of South Vietnam by the communists. She was left with a son then two years old and a daughter, five years old. She wanted desperately to flee their hometown, My-Tho. Several attempts to send her chil-dren to safety failed. In one attempt her son, then eight, was shot in the leg; a scar and reminder is still with him today. Tu and her children were eventually able to escape by boat, with the realiza-tion that if they were caught they would be killed. Luckily, they were rescued at sea after huddling cold and hungry for days just trying to survive. Three years at a refugee camp in Indonesia fol-lowed. Then they were sent to America.

They were relocated to central Los Angeles, California which is known for its gangs, poverty and violence. It was not the America they had dreamed of. Through word of mouth, Tu learned about the booming nail salon business. Speaking little English, Tu a for-mer teacher and dentist in Vietnam decided to train and enter the nail industry as soon as possible.

To safeguard her children from the negative environment of their neighborhood, she insisted that they remain with her in the nail salon after school to help her. Over her teen-age son's objection, Tu demanded that her son and daughter learn manicuring and nail care in the same way that many parents insist on piano les-sons for their children. Practice, practice, practice. Today her son counts those "forced lessons" as a blessing. He became a suc-cessful salon owner and later founded a nail academy in Virginia where others are taught the lessons he had learned.

Connections beyond the family

When Vietnamese nail techs and manicurists need supplies and equipment like nail polish or pedicure chairs, they naturally turn first to Vietnamese family members and friends who are on the vendors/supplier side of the nail industry. Further, there is peer pressure and community pressure to support others within the tight-knit Vietnamese community. On a practical level, when buying from other Vietnamese, communication is smooth as there is no written or spoken language barrier. Trust and trusting are factors embedded in Vietnamese heritage, religion and culture.

Who works in the salon?

Salon owner's often work in their salons. These owners do nails themselves and earn only from their own labor. Additional staff may consist of booth renters, employees or a combination of both. Other owners receive payment for booth rent plus they may take a percentage of service fees.

Owners may give employees a salary, a salary plus a percentage of service fees or compensation based on business volume. Many booth renters pay weekly. Other booth renters pay monthly. The average nail tech's income from service may be $420.00-$650.00 per week. Tips could bring in $129.00 with perhaps another $85.00 earned from retail sales. Hand lotion and nail polish are popular retail sales items. Other sales items include nail strengtheners/ nail treatments, top and base coats, nail files and buffers, skin and hair care products, jewelry, make up and cosmetics, candles, toe rings, purses, vitamins, clothing and gift items.

When additional staff is needed, eager relatives are often sponsored and recruited directly from Vietnam. Otherwise, when no family members are available, ads for nail techs are placed in local Vietnamese language newspapers. Positions are easy to fill. Working 10 hours per day with 1 hour per customer, a nail tech with little English can earn $100.00 per day or more, often paid in cash. She or he may work five to seven days per week. There are few benefits for sick leave, vacation or retirement. Still, salary, income and wages are much higher than is provided by employ-ment at Wal-Mart or McDonald's. Plus, there is more freedom in scheduling. This is perhaps enough to compensate nail techs for loss of time with their children, wiggly clients on cell phones, late clients or clients who fail to call or keep appointments.

Vietnamese nail salons generally do not advertise or market their businesses. Their clientèle is based upon the location of the busi-ness, its hours of operation, the specialties offered and the skill and friendliness of its staff. Clientèle is not based on the social integration of the Vietnamese owner's family into the neighbor-hood surrounding the business locale.

The profits from these salons when combined add up to Big Money for state and federal governments. According to nail industry 2012-2013 statistics, the nail industry grew to a record $7.47 bil-lion dollars during that time period.

Portrait of a manicurist/nail technician

A generalized portrait of a manicurist/nail tech can be drawn from available statistical data. In some categories, it is clear that research data collected may not reflect the precise extent to which the Vietnamese are proportionally represented in the statistics. For instance, race and ethnicity is not always tracked. So, while the data is not exact, it is helpful. The statistics come from on-line surveys of nail magazine readership, e-mailed surveys, monthly user polls, focus groups, and research data from the Bureau of Labor Statistics, U. S. Census, state cosmetology boards, and business license databases. Information has also been gathered from academic journals. First and foremost, 97% of the profession consists of females. On average the nail technician is 36-50 years old. Generally techs are married with kids although some are single parents. Even fewer are single with no children while some are married with no children. Many work part-time and previously held jobs other than nail tech.

Portrait of a nail salon owner – *Lynn's Nails*

Lynn's Nails is located in Aberdeen, a coastal city of 16,371 people. The salon is a three-hour drive traveling east from Seattle, Washington. Aberdeen has three nail salons. One is located in a small shopping mall which is anchored by a Sears store and a cinema complex. It is on the south side of town. The second salon is located in a strip mall next to a grocery store, Wal-Mart, Staples and Goodwill. It is on the north side of town. It is a very busy salon with a long tenure in its prime location. Directly across the street, facing the 4-way intersection is a sign. It is written on the side of a small, modest brown bungalow, one of few houses in the com-mercial district. The sign says *Lynn's Nails* in large blue letters.

Lynn's Nails offers manicures and pedicures only. I was a "walk-in". Lynn was alone but was expecting a customer at any moment, she said. She gave me an appointment to return two hours later that day. She didn't seem surprised when I showed up on time. Again, she was alone. Half of all salons have only one manicurist.

We talked during the procedure. Lynn is 35 years old, married and the mother of a six-year-old. She has owned Lynn's Nails for six years. It is her "day job." She loves her job because she can easily manage her schedule. She works five days a week, Tuesday through Saturday from 10 am until she finishes with her last customer. She has no employees. She works alone, although the salon has two manicure stations and two pedicure chairs. She has an alarm system for protection and does not fear for her safety.

Lynn went to college in Vietnam where she met and married her husband. He sponsored her to come to America. She likes America but enjoys returning home to Vietnam every two years or so to visit her parents, siblings and other relatives and to eat "home cooking." She also enjoys listening to Vietnamese music after work, and she pays extra to watch a Vietnamese language television station.

In addition to managing her own schedule, Lynn loves manicuring because it "is ladylike." If she ever decided to leave manicuring she would turn to fashion, "something with colors and styles or facials and skin care." She has no immediate plans to retire, how-ever. To stay current in her field, Lynn attends industry cosmetic shows and events to learn about the latest products, equipment, techniques and health and safety news. She also relies on sup-pliers to keep her informed about "the latest things." She has no health concerns.

Lynn says, "Some customers don't feel comfortable when another language is being spoken around them. I am the same way. I un-derstand." When her cell phone rang, Lynn answered and spoke in Vietnamese. She explained that it was her young daughter reporting she had a tummy ache.

Lynn was asked whether she noticed differences in black and white customers. She said that she has noticed that black ladies "tend to like the long nails whereas the white customers prefer the short nails." She adds, "I always follow what the customer wants and will make them happy." She puts the job first.

Lynn has also noticed that customers don't usually ask about her origin or ethnic background. "After being here for six years they just know me as a friend." As we spoke a customer came in and asked for an emergency nail repair. She was unhappy with the service she had received elsewhere but didn't want to make a fuss, so she came to Lynn for help. Lynn quickly scheduled her for later that evening.

Lynn does not know the history or origin of the nail salon business. She does know that she is glad that she has a nail salon business. Her parents in Vietnam are very proud of her.

Just as I was leaving, a different customer came in for a scheduled manicure. Lynn is staying busy!

Monique Nguyen Cosmetologist/manicurist

Monique Nguyen is 47 years old and is a self-employed cos-metologist and entrepreneur. Monique explains that she chose the French name for the convenience of her customers, but her Vietnamese friends call her Trang. She speaks fluent English which she learned in high school in Illinois and from practicing with clients. She was sponsored by and lived with her uncle when she came to America.

She had been sent by her parents with three younger siblings. Her parents had hopes that their children would get a better educa-tion and have a better life living in America. It was 1985. Ten years had passed since the fall of Saigon and the first waves of refugees arrived. Monique is an immigrant, not a refugee.

Monique's uncle and guardian urged her to study nursing after high school. He felt that would be a solid career for her. Out of obedience and family loyalty, she went to nursing school for two years. She complied with his wishes to set a good example for her younger siblings. Eager to be independent, she married. Her uncle had given permission for her marriage with the condition that she continue school after marriage. After her marriage Monique took a cosmetology course instead, loved it and never looked back.

Monique is a cosmetologist. As a cosmetologist, Monique is li-censed and trained to perform advanced skin, makeup, hair and nail beauty services. At first, when she got her license she avoided manicuring. So, for 10 years she was a hair stylist. Then, she moved to a city where the customers were seasonal snow-birds who wanted manicuring more often than hair-styling. To sustain her income, she switched to manicuring full-time.

"I didn't like it. There was always so much drama with customers complaining and co-workers bickering. Once I worked in a salon with 14 Vietnamese manicurists. It was a big salon. I was uncom-fortable there because of the manicurists' gossiping, in-fighting and jealousies about customer rotation. Somebody was always shit talking loud in Vietnamese when many customers just wanted quiet to relax. Sometimes they talked about their husbands, boyfriends and children. Sometimes they did whisper or mumble mean things about a customer if the customer didn't want to add to the basic service. I think that's rude. The customer just wants to get in and get out. It could be vicious."

Monique continues, "It isn't like that where I am now," she says.

"Now I've come to love my job and what I do. Every day is a new page, a new chapter with different people. I love the variety and the freedom. I'm the only Vietnamese in the salon, and I can talk to and enjoy my customers. They are my friends. They confide in me, tell me about their problems and their good times. It's kind of a therapy for them. Then they leave with their nails beautiful. We do charge a little more than some manicurists."

Monique says, "I have a customer that I admire very much. She is in her late 60s. She comes into the salon dressed in hip modern clothes, with her make-up and hair done. She is talkative, vibrant and friendly. I think she is a great role model. Her presence makes me feel happy."

"I had another customer. He had been referred to me. He had been given a gift certificate by his girlfriend. His feet were in very bad condition. I didn't show it in my manner. Instead I laughed and joked with him while I worked on his feet. When I was finished the bottoms of his feet were as soft as a new born baby's bottom! He appreciated what I had done for him and has been my customer ever since, about a year now. It really makes me feel good when my customer leaves happy."

Monique goes on, "Sometimes though things can become difficult. I have client and I love her personality. She takes a lot of medications for her health. She makes an appointment, then calls to cancel. I try to explain to her, we are friends but my work is a business. I am a single parent. If I cannot fill the time slot she has canceled on short notice, I lose money. Then, she cries. And she cries. I listen. I feel bad. I like her and don't want to lose her business."

Monique tells of another interesting experience. "One day a man came in. He was a nice man but he was huge, at least 500 pounds. I couldn't even raise the arms on the chair. He sat down and broke my pedicure chair! He apparently was embarrassed. He never came back."

Monique is divorced and has an 18-year-old son. He plans to pur-sue a career in bio-chemistry.

An Anonymous manicurist's story

"The grossest thing I have even done was a pedicure for an older woman of approximately 60 something. Her toenails grew upwards like horns instead of straight out like normal due to an extreme nail fungus that was never treated. Her toes were all squished together due to years of wearing pointed toed heels when she was younger (yes they ruin your feet). While I was doing her pedicure, in order to cut her toenails I had to use a grinder in order to cut them down, due to the thickness. I ended up getting a mask so I didn't continue to breathe the nail dust in. She can't cut her own toenails and only has enough money to come in once a year, so they were very long and very thick. Also in between her toes, was a green putrid liquid-like fungus that I had to personally wipe out with my hands because if you did it with anything else her skin started to bleed. Her skin was so raw and sensitive from the fungus, and from her toes never being able to air out and dry in between each other, because they were squished together."

The manicurist concluded her story, "I felt horrible for her, but also for myself. So, yes, worst and grossest feet EVER!"

Vietnamese author and manicurist, Lan Ton shares fictional stories about working in a nail salon in her book *Got My Nails Did*.

Colors and genders

The vast majority of nail techs are female. From an ethnic standpoint over half of nail techs are Vietnamese. Caucasians represent the next largest group. This is followed by Blacks, then by Hispanics and lastly by other ethnic groups, like the Koreans in the New York salons. Most techs have been doing nails for more than 10 years. A nail technician/manicurist license requires less money and fewer education hours than a cosmetology license.

That is why the manicurist license is held by the majority of nail technician/manicurists. Cosmetologists can do hair, nails and other services not permitted by techs. Estheticians focus on skin care but can also provide manicures.

Work-related injury

Nail techs like most people who perform physical work have some work-related health issues. In fact, a majority experience work-related health issues. Almost half report back problems. A large percentage also report neck, shoulder and wrist problems. Not surprisingly, many techs have experienced repetitive stress or carpal tunnel syndrome. Ironically, few techs use preventative measures such as wearing gloves, using finger wraps, wearing a wrist brace, respirator face mask, protective eye-wear or splash-resistant clothing.

However, when a tech becomes pregnant she may cease working in order to protect an unborn fetus from potential chemical fume damage. Chemicals like methyl methacrylate have been used but are now outlawed because of potential reproductive and cancer health hazards to nail salon workers. Although products may have pretty names like, "Pink Champagne" nail salon workers also face exposure to other chemicals, such as formaldehyde, toluene, and dibutyl phthalate. Fortunately, a good number of nail techs have medical insurance and some have professional liability insurance, as well.

Vietnamese male manicurists

Asian males are rarely shown in American movies or on television. Even in modern times Asian males are stereotyped as skilled in karate, and little else. In the past, they have been shown in films as mere houseboys for Caucasian male employers. In the Peter Seller's 1964 film, *A Shot in the Dark* an Asian male, Burt Kwouk, is portrayed as both. No wonder, it took a while for some female customers to accept a male doing their nails. Vietnamese male manicurists/techs are in the minority in the largely female-dominated industry.

There are fewer, if any, male techs in the Vietnam homeland due to cultural taboos concerning subservience of women. Many Vietnamese-American male immigrants chose to overcome those taboos in order to find work and make money. Many left behind careers in science, teaching, and the military. They, like females, faced racial discrimination in employment, inability to provide proof of professional degrees and certificates and insufficient
English language skill. So, they turned to manicuring.

This was true for Regal Nails founder, "Charlie" Guy Ton who found no work as a chemical engineer. He first turned to nail product distribution but there were too few salons at that time. He then chose to work at his wife's salon. Finally, he turned to nail salon franchising, which reportedly made him a millionaire.

One young male manicurist said, "A job is a job." Another one said, "A job is a job and I see a lot of hot chicks!"

John Ngo

John's story is not uncommon. He was 16 when he made his first escape attempt from a labor camp in Vietnam. "I was caught, beaten and brought back." He made 14 more escape attempts. Finally, he was successful and made his way to a nearby country's refugee camp where he languished for several years before com-ing to America, alone. By working two or more menial jobs at one time, John was able to save enough money to train in manicuring. He was so good so fast and so meticulous that the beauty school quickly hired him as an instructor.

John is a naturalized citizen now and owns his own salon where he employees several nail techs. Over time, as a result of his ef-forts he was able to bring his mother and brothers to America. John like many others felt that the way to prosperity was to be an entrepreneur having his own business. In addition to his nail salon, John also owns a gold-buying business.

Most popular services and prices

At nail salons, manicures and pedicures are by far the most popu-lar service. During the course of a week a nail tech may perform 12 acrylic fills and full sets, 2 sets of gel toe nails, 9 gel polish ap-plications, 9 pedicures and 9 manicures. Gel services cost twice the price of a regular manicure or pedicure. That's because gel applications can last up to two weeks. An addition of glitter can increase the price even more.

In the beginning nail salons offered services for "nails only." This usually included the manicure, the pedicure and simple painted designs such as flowers or stars. By the 1980s acrylic nail exten-sions became available. The acrylic nail "full set" is what took the Vietnamese nail salon to the "next level" in industry dominance.

Vietnamese and non-Vietnamese nail techs flooded the market to take advantage of the new beauty trend. But, the Vietnamese offered the best service prices from a customer's point of view.

Like self-propagating plants, Vietnamese nail technicians have spread out across the United States. They did so in order to escape fierce competition, raise service prices or simply to relocate nearer family members. While it is true that fierce competition drives down service prices, it also greatly expands the market. A nail salon on almost every street is also great free advertising. This strategy was not planned by any Madison Ave corporate mar-keting department; it was simply the result of individual owners' decisions to disperse.

The result, as they spread out made affordable nail care accessible to ordinary women-the masses. The more people wanted a manicure, the more products were needed to be manufactured and distributed. The Vietnamese manicure is therefore the founda-tion of the now dynamic nail care market which was once dormant.

Nail salons dropped their service prices to compete with others in the industry. Lowering prices was not a good response to the heavy competition. Vietnamese nail salons then began expand-ing their beauty services to include skin care and application of make-up. They are also incorporating new techniques, methods and technologies. Nail salons now specialize in acrylics, fiber-glass, paraffin, UV top coats, silk wraps, gels, air brushing and reflexology therapeutic massage.

To distinguish his salon Glamour Nails from other salons in the Detroit area, owner Quarter Dihn the "Singing Manicurist" special-izes by entertaining his clients with Karaoke. "It's about making them happy," he says. He sang, "Achy Breaky Nails" on YouTube and has appeared on American Idol.

In striving for innovation some salons went too far. California has banned a pedicure service which remains popular in Turkey and the Far East. Fish pedicures are no longer an option in California. This pedicure treatment consisted of the use of live small imported Garra Rufa or Chin Chin fish to nibble dead skin off the feet to smooth the soles. This procedure was banned because there was no way to disinfect the fish or the water for re-use. Also, it was rumored that some of the imported fish had teeth so sharp they could draw blood.

Service prices going up or going down

Without question, the Vietnamese revitalized the nail care industry. Yet, for decades the nail industry has endured flat service prices. For instance, in the last 20 years there have been price increases only in basic manicures, basic pedicures and acrylic fills. In 1992 manicures were about $11.00 dollars. In 2012 the cost was roughly $20.00. Likewise pedicures were $22.00 in 1992. They are now $32.00. These results show lack of inflation-adjusted increases or lack of supplemental services which would increase income and profit opportunity.

Payment for services

Now only half of nail techs take walk-in clients without an appoint-ment. Appointments are preferred. During the course of a week a tech may service 5-50 clients. Many techs use the three strikes and you're out system for clients who consistently fail to show up for appointments. Many clients pay for services with cash. Others use credit, debit cards or write a check. A very small number of techs bill their clients.

Female customers

Many women visit a nail salon seasonally or in preparation for a special occasion. On the other end of the spectrum, some women visit a nail salon weekly. Women 55 years or older are the biggest spenders on professional nail services. Many clients who were once conservative now sport trendy new colors and designs on their fingers. Color is not just hidden away on their toes. These clients are generally referred by word-of-mouth since nail salons spend very little on paid advertising. Friday is the busiest day of the week at salons which may open at 10 A.M. and close well after 7:00 P.M.

It is unusual for a customer to be turned away even after closing time because competition within the industry is fierce. It does hap-pen however. According to newspaper accounts, service has been refused to some men, the obese, and an AIDS victim. Service has not been refused to those wearing electronic ankle monitoring bracelets courtesy of the criminal justice system.

Sometimes there is conflict. One woman called 911 because she didn't like the length or shape of her nails. Other instances of customers behaving badly have been recorded. These instances include loud-talking, cursing, brawling and even arrests made in service-satisfaction disputes.

Racial mecca

As has been mentioned, beauty shops have a racially segmented history. Blacks traditionally have their own shops and whites have their own shops. However, there is at least one nail salon business in the United States, "Mantrap Nail & Hair" which is co-owned since 1979 by a Vietnamese woman Charlie Vo and an African-American woman, Olivett Robinson. Together they own seven shops.

Over all nail salons are still unique because the workers and customers come from distinctly different racial and cultural backgrounds. Customers sit side by side holding the hands of a Vietnamese tech. The close proximity of seating does not promote social intermingling, however. In some suburbs the customers may be all Caucasian and the techs all Vietnamese. Korean Sociologist, Milliann Kang noted that many middle and upper class white customers have a sense of entitlement. They want ex-tra massages and pampering. They also take the nail tech's time to express their plans and troubles.

Closer to the inner city, particularly at shopping malls, custom-ers represent the full spectrum of racial and ethnic composition. Kang noted that African Americans and working-class customers want respect, fast service and reasonable prices. In both situa-tions, very few customers inquire into the nationality, background or family of the manicurist. No recognition or distinction is made regarding ethnic identity, whether the tech is Japanese, Chinese, Vietnamese or Korean. The tech is merely "Asian."

What are nail techs talking about in Vietnamese?

Many customers wonder if nail techs are talking about them when they converse with each other in Vietnamese. Anh Do, a reporter who understood Vietnamese went undercover in a salon to file a newspaper article about their conversations. According to the Los Angeles Times article, nail techs speak in Vietnamese about their children, husbands, boyfriends, and occasionally may comment on a customer. One tech commented that a customer must play cards because she had rough skin or *"ban tay cua nguoi danh bai"* —gambler's hands."

Their comments and observances are not often mean although they can be. Even so, it is hard to imagine anyone could work a full 8-hour shift without speaking to a co-worker. Furthermore, not all English speaking customers are discreet in their comments about nail techs that they assume will not understand their words or see them roll their eyes.

Customer loyalty

Customers give a number of reasons for their loyalty to a nail salon and nail technician. The reasons go beyond mere reasonable service prices. Reasons include: They do a good job; they are friendly; they accept walk-ins; the tech speaks English; the salon is located in the customer's neighborhood and shopping area; the service is fast, 30-45 minutes rather than 1 hour elsewhere. Over all convenience and customer service seem to be the "bottom line."

The male customer

In sophisticated urban areas there are usually some heterosexual males given to enhancing personal appearance by fastidious grooming, beauty treatments, and fashionable clothes. They are the metrosexuals. Of course, there are also male entertainers who proudly display nail art.

Generally, today's male customer is rare and likely over 45 years old. One customer even reported being rejected because of his gender. Another customer filed a lawsuit charging discrimination because he was charged $1 more for a manicure compared to the price charged women for the same service. Men are welcome at Vietnamese nail salons.

To capture the emerging male market, there are also non-Vietnamese salons like San Francisco's Spargo. Los Angeles has Hammer and Nails which offers an ultimate sleek "Man Cave." Amenities there include female manicurists, king-size leather chairs, personal flat-screen TVs with headphones and premium sports channels. Tempe Arizona has Nails by Males. This men-only nail salon is by and for males. Osaka, Japan also has men-only salons like Men's Nail Unique where male "nailists" service male businessmen who see a manicure as proper etiquette. Men there receive services such as nail trimming, filing and shaping for nails on hands and feet. Massage is also provided.

Around the Country-Regional Analysis

All 50 states have Vietnamese nail salons. California ranks number one with the most nail technicians and nail salons. In 2013 it was reported that California had ninety thousand nail techs and six thousand salons. Hollywood, California has long been known as an image-conscious area. There the new nail beauty routine fits into the flamboyant aura. The aura appeals to the masses who are eager to emulate the glamorous and the elite. What better state to ignite the nail salon craze than California?

After all, the 20 women who were the original Vietnamese nail techs started in California. As the trade developed, beauty schools were needed to meet the needs of the growing nail markets.
Vietnamese beauty schools soon flourished in California, espe-cially Little Saigon in Orange County. Little Saigon, a three-square-mile area, is a bustling community of 4000 restaurants, shops and other Vietnamese businesses including beauty schools. Advance
Beauty College was one of the first.

The trade and nail salons then spread nationwide. Texas has the second highest number of techs and salons. Florida ranks third. Interestingly, the state of South Dakota has the least number of techs and salons. In total there were 364,247 nail techs in the United States in 2013 with 48,930 salons.

Chapter 5

HEADLINES-RUMORS-ACCUSATIONS AND STEREOTYPES

Like all businesses, nail salons are subject to scrutiny from both public and private sources. Licensing agencies, customers and newspapers offer a glimpse into nail salon operations. The headlines which follow were taken from major newspapers around the country.

Nail Salons and Human Trafficking.

How Safe is Your Nail Salon?

Safety Campaign Tries to Re-shape Nail Salons.

Nail Salon Employee Now Charged with Sexual Assault.

Finger-Pointing Over Sickening Fumes.

Letter Campaign Targets Nail Salons.

Gunman Robs 3 Inside Wilmette Nail Salon.

Foreign Retailers Should Adapt.

South Pasadena Puts the Bite on Nail Salons.

A Cashmere Coat Valued at $1000 Was Reported Stolen at a Nail Salon.

Newport Beach: Stricter Parking Rule for Nail Salons Okd.

A Need for Rating System for Nail Salons.

Pointing a Finger at Discount Nail Salons.

How Did Tippi Hedren Launch the Vietnamese Nail Salon Industry?

Women Bonding in Nail Salon: A Place Lost in Time.

The California Nail Polish Scandal and What it Means for Your Manicure.

Multi-Colored Nails: Saving Grace or Trendy Waste?

Sick for Beauty: Protect the Health of Nail Salon Workers!

Polishing the American Dream: Vietnamese Nail Salons are Spread Throughout South Florida.

Bad Manicures-Nail Salon Risks.

Hot Springs Nail Salon Denies Woman Pedicure Because of Her Weight.

New Regulation Could Put Many Nail Salons Out of Business, Lawmaker Says.

Do Nail Salon Workers Have a Higher Incidence of Cancer?

Man Contracts Life-Threatening Infection at Nail Salon.

Friends Remember Mother Killed in Her Own Nail Salon.

A Grooming Ritual Nails Down a Friendship.

Mother Gives Her Daughter a Hand.

Nail Salons Wring Hands at Odor Rule.

Owner's Slaying Shatters Spirit at Nail Salon.

Oakland Looks at Trimming Number of Nail Salons.

Fingers Do the Talking.

Maywood Man Gets 45 Years for Bellwood Nail Salon Robbery.

A Martini With Your Manicure?

NY Nail Salon Refuses Service Based on Gender.

Officer Shot When Gun Accidentally Discharges in South Shore Nail Salon.

Vietnamese Nail Niche Business.

Nail-Salon Robber is clipping up a Storm.

The Grand Prize is a Visit to Your Favorite Nail Salon.

Marilyn Monroe Nail Salons, Cafe in the Works.

Nail Salons' Gloss Is Worn Thin by Economic Woes.

Nail Care Basics for Men.

Mani-Pedi add-ons: Are They Worth It?

Charges Against Salon in AIDS Case Dropped.

A Time for Big Decisions in Little Saigon.

Diving Feet First into a Pedicure.

Arsonist Given 11 Years for Salon Fires.

Nail Salon Named in AIDS Bias Case Cites Health Fears.

Nail Services a Point of Popularity.

Getting Your Nails Done in a Manly Manner.

Court Asked to Order Nail Salon to Serve AIDS Victim.

Santa Monica Starts Program to Make Nail Salons Safer.

In Good Hands? As Nail Salons Proliferate, So Do Health Problems.

Industry Watchers Worry About Unsafe Conditions, Unlicensed Operators.

Bill Targets Nail Salon Outbreaks.

Newport Beach: Council to scrutinize Nail Salon Parking.

Man Who Set Himself on Fire in Nail Salon Not Expected to Survive.

L.A.'s Latest Manicure-Pedicure Spots Nail the Spa-Boutique Vibe.

Improperly Sanitized Nail Salon Equipment Can Cause Infection.
Local Nail Salons Fined for Using Dangerous MMA Chemicals.
Could You Be Risking Your Health at a Nail Salon?
Unsanitary Conditions Rife in Nail Salons.
City Council Seeks to Limit the Number of Nail Salons in the City.

These headlines perhaps reveal tension in the Vietnamese and non-Vietnamese nail care communities. Allegations have been made that Asian salons hurt the "legitimate" nail care profession. Cited are alleged salon problems with questionable products, damage to nails, unlicensed technicians, poor sanitation and lack of client communication. Allegations are also made that the Vietnamese purchase supplies only from other Vietnamese. However, it remains unclear the extent to which non-Vietnamese purchase supplies from Vietnamese suppliers and vendors.

One Vietnamese nail salon owner indicated that he thought Vietnamese nail salons were unfairly singled out for negative criticism. In comparison, negative comments published about barbershops and beauty salons are almost never expressed. Dr. Tam Nguyen, beauty college owner and cosmetology advocate, agrees that, "Problems do happen in all aspects of the beauty industry in high end affluent areas and in every ethnic and socio-economic group, yet nail salon problems overwhelmingly get the majority of the bad press."

The disproportionate media attention fuels tension within the industry. "Communication is still lacking and it takes compassion and caring to bridge the gap," according to Dr. Nguyen. In fact, most of the complaints about nail salons come not from customers but from competitors within the industry. Only when a customer files a complaint with the state will an inspector go out to investigate. Most states have only 10-15 inspectors and are not able to confirm or deny general allegations.

English language newspapers and academic journals have no record of Vietnamese making negative comments about the non-Vietnamese in the nail industry. Dan Hoang, publisher of the 60,000 subscription Vietnamese-language trade magazine *Saigon Nails* acknowledges that there is a communication gap between Vietnamese and American nail technicians which causes alienation. *Saigon Nails* helps to fill that void by communicating nail industry news about education, practices and tips. *NAILS MAGAZINE*, represents 55,000 subscribers in the nail industry. The small advertisement filled Vietnamese-language section of *NAILS MAGAZINE* is called *VietSalon*.

The nail industry continues to grow based on the hard work, persistence, creativity and innovation of its members. The Vietnamese, like other immigrants, give many reasons for owning businesses. They cite lack of fluent language skills, home country educational credentials not being recognized by American companies and experiencing racial discrimination. Their motivations for business ownership include a desire for independence and a desire to put knowledge, training and experience to work.

Other motivators include achieving personal freedom and satisfaction from growth and job security. The factors contributing to their businesses' success, they believe, include friendliness to customers, charisma and very hard work. Family support is a major contributing factor for them. Other factors include a good location for the business, good training and skill development along with good customer service. Going forward they see the following as problems: excessive competition within the industry, insufficient management training, unsafe salon locations, discrimination from customers and unreliable employees.

Despite these limitations the nail industry continues to enjoy increased popularity fueled by past and present products and services. Salon customer numbers have increased. Service prices have increased. New services have increased. New products have increased. Social media use has increased. These activities help indirectly to create jobs for nail focused manufacturers and beauty suppliers as well as for nail techs and salon owners. As a result nail salons are important to the American economy.

Significant economic contributions come from the nail industry and from other immigrant business entrepreneurs. These businesses generate at least 67 billion of the 577 billion in U.S. business income. They employ 12% of the total U.S. workforce.

Chapter 6

CELEBRITY CULTURE

At one time, colored nail polish was considered by psychiatrists to be unhealthy, and polishing one's nails was thought to be a form of self-mutilation. Despite this, the First Lady of the United States of America to wear nail color was Eleanor Roosevelt. Sales of lavender colored nail polish soared after it was worn by Michelle Obama at the Democratic National Convention. Other celebrity endorsements include those of Nicki Minaj, Carrie Underwood,
Selena Gomez, Maria Carey, the Kardashians and several female Olympians. Drug store sales of polish and nail products have jumped. Polish sales alone are up 59%. Sales numbers of other natural nail products are up 36% with a 100% increase in top and base coats.

Nail Artist Celebrities

In the recently released film *The Wolf of Wall Street* nail art was as closely watched as the costumes worn by the actors. Hollywood manicurist to the stars **Gina Eppolito** created the film's distinctive 90s-inspired look for the nails of each character. The nail designs highlighted bold colors, rhinestones and French manicures with long square tips.

Japanese artist **Naomi Yasuda**, the personal manicurist to Lady GaGa, developed and designed the Lady GaGa brand of stick-on nails. Naomi attended the Chunichi Beauty College in Nagoya, Japan.

Trang Nguyen is an internationally known Vietnamese nail artist and the inventor of the Odyssey Nail System (ONS). He also competes in nail art competitions worldwide. As an instructor-trainer he inspires nail techs to be passionate about their work.

Robbie Schaeffer is a well-known celebrity manicurist who caters to the Hollywood crowd. He is the son of O.P.I (Odontorium Products Inc.) founder George Schaeffer. O.P.I is associated with COTY, Inc.

Dzine, a Puerto Rico immigrant and Chicago area artist has also received acclaim for his nail art installations which have been fea-tured in several museums. He is not a manicurist. His exhibitions have been included in Brooklyn Museum of Art collections, the Museo Del Barrio in New York; the Bass Museum of Art in Miami and the Museum of Contemporary Art in Chicago.

Pamela Council's sculpture is made of hand-painted nail tips set on a wood base. The piece called Flo Jo World Record Nails references the Olympic world records won by athlete Florence Griffith-Joyner who was known for wearing colorful long fingernails.

Prize-winning Vietnamese manicurist **Johnny Nam Kiet**, 29, for five years has run one of London's most popular nail academies. "Nearly everyone who graduates here goes to work abroad. I just train them," he stated in *Post Magazine*. Johnny is also a prominent clothing designer.

British entrepreneur **Thea Green,** who is Caucasian, founded Nails, Inc. in 1999 at the age of 23. She shared her story with the UK's Huffington Post. "As a youth, I wanted to earn my own money and always talked about having my own business," she says. She was inspired to open nail bars after seeing and using nail salons in New York while traveling as a fashion editor. She took the idea and the trend back home. Her company now employs 420 people with 58 nail bars in Ireland and the United Kingdom.

Thea, 36, is married and the mother of three small children.

Social Media and Sales

Social media is widely used by nail techs. Eighty percent have personal and business Facebook pages. Many also have a Twitter account, a YouTube channel, a Four Square page, a Pinterest Board, an Instagram account and a LinkedIn account. On Instagram and Pinterest nail art is among the most tagged items.

Over half of nail salons have websites. Facebook and Twitter sites are used to share and display nail art created by techs and worn by clients. In this way nail designs by the thousands are shared. In addition, there are numerous blogs about nail techniques, nail polish and nail art. In fact, on the Internet there are more than 25 million monthly searches for the term *nail art.*

The sales market has been fueled by social media's spreading the word about innovative techniques for applying products. Women in the mass market are inspired by designs they can create with nail polish. Back in the day, nail polish was available only at drug stores and a few retail stores. But today, nail polish can be bought everywhere goods are sold. In the past, when times get rough, women bought a new lipstick as a mood pick-me-up. Now a woman buys a new nail polish instead. During the best of times a woman buys several nail polish colors or she may visit a salon. This fact has been referred to as the "polish index" of economic conditions.

Innovations and Spin-offs

From acrylic nail to silk wrap to gel nail, all of these forms involve use of chemicals. To address this issue, advancements are continually being made to provide safer chemicals and ventilation systems. In fact a "green certification" has been developed to distinguish businesses that implement products, technologies, methods and procedures that are eco-friendly. Nonetheless, the iconic acrylic nail full-set is now decreasing in demand.

Nail Polish to Gel Polish

A female French make-up artist produced what was later called nail polish. Nail polish started out with colors available primarily in pink, red, purple, clear or black. An infinite variety of colors is now available. In addition to solid colors, there are also nail polish stamps, crackled finishes, strips and stickers. Fake rhinestones can be applied. The world's most expensive nail polish contained 267 carats of black diamonds. The polish cost $250,000. For a mere $30, an 18 karat White Gold and Silver Leaf Topcoat is available.

There are "Boutique" brands like Nars, Butter London and Rescue Beauty and there are humble Dollar Store brands. Polishes are also being marketed to men. In addition, there is a market for pol-ishes that provide more than beauty. These polishes are designed to encourage nail growth and to make the nail stronger, to prevent splitting or breaking. There is even a nail polish to discourage nail biting.

Gel polish has increased in popularity due to its durability. A manicure with gel polish can last up to two weeks without flaking, peeling or becoming dull in color. Gel polish is not just the trend; it's also an industry standard. It has revolutionized the nail industry just as acrylic nail extensions did decades earlier. Refinements are being made almost daily in gel polish and in techniques for its application and safe removal. There's no end to the array of colors available. Fifty or more brands feed this hungry market.

Brands include magnetic and mood changing gels and polishes, nail appliqués, real lacquer strips, caviar nails and holographic color. UVs, combination UV/LED, LED, 2-hand and 1-finger lamps have come on the market to cure the polish. Some polishes are specifically formulated to be compatible with a lamp provided by the manufacturer. The best results are said to be achieved using the manufacturer's lamp.

DID YOU KNOW?

Acrylic nail extensions were first invented and patented by a dentist.

Greek women once wore empty pistachio shells as nail extensions.

Musicians like guitarist James Taylor use nail extensions to protect their nails and to produce special guitar sounds.

Tennis star Serena Williams has a manicuring license and demonstrated her skills giving Oprah a pedicure.

Ancient Chinese noblewomen wore nail extensions.

There are international competitions for nail art design.

Film maker Adele Phan is developing a documentary about nail salons.

Oprah Winfrey's cable network (OWN) has planned a season One 2014-2015 reality TV show based on 18 nail artists competing for a $100,000 prize. The show is called Nail'd It.

Nail salons are located in major airports like Seattle's SeaTac International Airport.

Nail salons are located in many Wal-Mart stores.

Some nail salons have as many as 100 pedicure chairs.

One Vietnamese salon owner has 99 salons.

Vietnamese nail salons are in almost every country.

Vietnam now has mobile manicurists who reach customers by bicycle.

Nail salons are located in American high-end retail stores like Bloomingdale's.

Nail salons are located in five-star hotels world-wide.

Texas has a large Vietnamese equipment manufacturing plant.

A nail bar in the Beverly Wilshire Hotel, located near Rodeo Drive, offers what clients expect from a "Beverly Hills" experience.

There are male only nail salons with male manicurists.

There are waterless pedicure treatments.

Vietnamese manicurist Lan Ton is the author of *Got My Nails Did*, fictional stories about working in a nail salon.

Mobile nail salons travel to homes in New York neighborhoods.

The reality show *Nail Files* focuses on the personal and professional life of Katie Czorla, a Caucasian nail salon entrepreneur living in Hollywood. The show premiered in 2011.

Specialty nail polish is available for the pampered dog.

Salon to Boutique to Spa

A boutique is generally a small business offering specialized services and products. It holds a mid-level position between a salon and a spa including elements from both. Boutique services are priced lower but are delivered in a higher-end environment. Specialized services may include waxing, eyebrow shaping, acrylic toenails, nail art, foot massage, silk or linen wrap, and make-up application. Additional services might include fiberglass wraps, massage and reflexology, eyelash extensions, eyelash tinting, facials, or emergent waterless pedicure-medical treatment for diabetes. Customized salon products are for retail sale.

From Simple Manicure to Art Form

A manicure simply involves cuticle removal, shaping and filing the nails, a hand massage and polishing the nail to a glossy finish. This is how the nail as a canvas is prepared. From that point on, nail art becomes an artistic creative process open to the imagination and skill of the nail tech/manicurist. Techniques and procedures are varied and designs are infinite. The finished product is the creative expression of both the manicurist and the customer who requests and wears it. Nail art is fashion, wearable fashion. The nail extension or the natural nail may be shaped to be pointed, square, oval or round. Stripes, dots, or intricate 3-D designs are all possible using novel techniques involving paint, polish, air-guns, brushes, decals, stickers, glitter and gems. Delicate patterns on a French manicure base have evolved for bridal wear. Nail designs are for all seasons and all trends.

Nail art is one service which is increasing nail salon profitability. Most nail technicians charge for adding nail art. The price may depend upon the complexity of the design and the type of art. Service may involve a flat rate or a different rate per nail, per color. Some technicians do not charge for nail art. *Cosmopolitan Magazine* in the UK calls nail art the biggest U.S. beauty export of the last decade. This phenomenon is attributed to the savvy UK Vietnamese community who are playing a big part in their nail art obsession largely in edgy east and south London. Street manicurists even offer the Mani-Pedi by the roadside. Armed with their toolkit and two plastic stools they sell locals and tourists their services for pence.

National Nail Art Competitions

America's *NAILS Magazine* sponsors a national nail art competition. The contest winner receives the title NAILS Next Top Nail Artist. The United Kingdom's WorldSkills organization also hosts a national nail art competition. The competition has various levels of difficulty. At each level competitors are required to demonstrate and create a finished product which reflects standards of beauty, knowledge of current fashion trends and artistic design. India held its first nail art competition in 2014. Nail technicians from all over India competed at the StyleSpeak Nailathon. Germany and Ireland host national nail competitions as well.

International Competitions

Trang Nguyen inventor of the Odyssey Nail System (ONS) competes in and trains artists for nail art competitions worldwide including events in: Korea, Kuala Lumpur, Japan, Australia, New Zealand and Singapore. Additionally, WorldSkills is the largest interna-tional skills competition in the world. The last Worldskills competi-tion was held in Leipzig, Germany. The competition is held every two years in cities around the globe. Winners receive a medal. EuroSkills is a bi-biennial competition for member countries in Europe. These competitions allow competitors to hone their skills for international events.

International Business from local to global

The cost of a manicure is included in the British government's key inflation indexes. That's how popular manicures have become in Britain and many other countries. After the fall of Saigon,

Vietnamese immigrants who fled were resettled in several countries who had agreed to receive them. The United States, Britain, Australia and Canada were among the host countries. Vietnamese families were dispersed throughout these countries and many were reunited only by their own efforts after many years apart. As they visited family and friends in the United States, they took home with them the nail salon business model, the "Vietnamese nail salon." In Britain they are called "nail bars." One multi-national business franchise owned by Guy "Charlie" Ton has 1000 salons located in Wal-Mart stores alongside Subway and McDonald's. Those salons are located throughout the U. S., Canada and Puerto Rico. Nail salons have no corporate shareholders. Instead thou-sands of individual entrepreneurs own small salons worldwide including Prague, Japan, France and Germany.

Nail Salons Now In Vietnam

The nail salon was made in the USA, started by Vietnamese refugees. Vietnamese who live outside of Vietnam are called the Viet Kieu. The Viet Kieu started visiting their homeland after 1994 when the United States lifted its trade embargo. Some returned to Vietnam to visit relatives and to savor the fruits and vegetables of their native country. Some visited Vietnam to experience the land of their parents and ancestors.

The first nail salons were started in Vietnam by families who had Viet Kieu connections. Nail salons have since spread to the capital city of Hanoi and beyond. Office workers and trend-setting youth are the targeted clientèle. Clients also include foreigners and the wealthy who prefer that the manicurist make a home visit.

High-spending tourists can take advantage of the five-star Shine Hotel and Spa at Sheraton Nha Trang, Vietnam. The Spa there offers a Deluxe Manicure and Pedicure plus massage services. A guest may select from the Shine Vietnamese Massage-Indian Head Therapy-Arabian Executive Back Massage-Oriental Four Hand Massage (which includes 2 therapists working on the body at the same time)-Oriental Foot Therapy or the Mediterranean Hot Stone Treatment.

The high-end market is catered to by manicurists with pro-fessional training and artistic talent.

On the other, low end of the market, are the manicure peddlers who are the lowest ranked among manicurists in Vietnam. A mani-cure peddler meets clients as they travel from street to street on foot, bicycle or motorbike carrying a small bag of supplies. They offer simple services like trimming nails. Their clients are small vendors, shopkeepers in stalls or small markets. If the client is busy with a customer, the manicurist returns later. At this level of availability everyone has access to some form of manicure, and even the least skilled can earn a meager livelihood.

Manicure training in Vietnam

The more skilled and experienced manicurists in Vietnam ac-quired knowledge and training from Viet Kiev family members, established beauty shops and nail salons or from courses taken in the United States. At The Women's Cultural House in Ho Chi Minh City, youth can learn the manicuring trade along with cosmetol-ogy, cooking and flower arranging. Many will have job offers even before they complete their courses. Some will train in preparation for owning their own nail shops or for working in America or for going to other countries to work in family-owned salons.

Many native Vietnamese take manicuring classes alongside Viet Kiev in beauty schools in Vietnam where manicure training classes are far less expensive than training classes in other countries. Manicuring supplies like files, clippers, chairs and other tools of the trade are much less expensive when purchased in Vietnam. A complete set of tools could cost from $140 to $600 depending upon quality. Tools include polishes, glosses, sanitizers, emery boards, files and brushes. The Vietnamese have established beauty schools with manicuring courses in other countries, like Japan.

Newton Lu, CEO of LeChat Nail Care Products says that, "Vietnam is still a virgin market for nail care."

Chapter 7

WHERE ARE THEY NOW?

TIPPI HEDREN

Tippi Hedren is quite a woman. Born as Nathalie Kay Hedren, "Tippi" is 82 years old today. She is renowned for her acting career and other accomplishments. In September 2013 she received the Legacy of Style Award. At the well-attended event, Tippi Hedren was named the "Godmother" of Vietnamese-American nail salons. She was not at Hope Village in 1975 for a photo opportunity to merely be seen as helping the women. She was there as a volun-teer. She was there to help and she did help. She remains in close contact with many of the women today.

Thuan Le and Yen Rist, two of the original manicurists, have recounted in the foregoing pages Tippi's numerous acts of kind-ness, inspiration, encouragement and business savvy. The 18 other women would no doubt add their voices to the chorus of ac-colades had they been available for comment and participation in the writing of this book. She is known to have given each woman her full attention.

Thuan Le and several of the original 20 women were present at the 2nd Annual Legacy of Style Award presented by Creative Nail Design (CND) and a Los Angeles organization called Beauty Changes Lives (BCL). Tippi Hedren received the award for her contributions to the professional nail industry. The two groups established a nail scholarship in her honor. Vidal Sassoon was the 2012 recipient of the prestigious award.

Over the years Tippi has continuously been recognized for her quick wit and perception of the career needs of the 20 immigrant women. In 2013 she also received the People Helping People award from the Touching Lives TV Award Show. Prior to that time, in 2003 Tippi was awarded the annual Hope is a Woman award by the Women of Los Angeles. She received the Women Together award presented by the United Nations in 2011. In 2011 she also received the Vietnamese-American Martin Saint award from the Boat People SOS Organization.

Tippi was quoted in *A Celebration of Women* saying that she became friends with the 20 Vietnamese women whom she grew to love so dearly. She feels honored to have taken part in their success in the manicuring business. "I am in awe of how successful they have become," she stated.

Tippi Hedren. Photo by Araya-Diaz/Getty Images
for Creative Nail Design 2013

Tippi Hedren with a baby leopard. Photo autographed to
Thuan Le.

Tippi Hedren's compassion extends to animals as well. She is known and recognized for founding the Shambala Preserve an 80-acre California property where Tippi cares for lions, tigers and other wildlife. Michael Jackson's two Bengal tigers, Sabu and Thriller made their home there after Jackson closed his zoo. Tippi currently directs the Roar Foundation which manages the Shambala Preserve. In addition to her humanitarian work, Tippi Hedren is well known for her role in Alfred Hitchcock's film *The Birds* and the later film *Marnie*.

She has appeared in 50 movies and numerous TV shows for which she has received many achievement awards from the film industry. She has a star on the Hollywood Walk of Fame. Tippi made another notable contribution to the film industry. She is the mother of actress Melanie Griffith. Tippi is also the grandmother of actress Dakota Johnson, star of the film *Fifty Shades of Grey*.

The first 20 Licensed Vietnamese manicurists in the
UnitedStates. 1975

20 WOMEN

There were several types of refugees in 1975 at Hope Village. Many were former farm workers who could not read or write even in their native language, Vietnamese. Among the refugees were 20 Vietnamese women who spoke little English but were former teachers, business owners and government officials. Three were wives of generals. Some of them had lost their husbands in the Vietnam War. They had no marketable skills. They were nonetheless an elite group by virtue of their education, background and experience. For this reason they were singled out to participate in the manicure training Tippi provided through her personal manicurist. Later the women studied at the Cyprus Heights Beauty College. After graduation from Beauty College, many of the women like Thuan Le and Yen Rist were able to sustain careers in manicur-ing. Some, however, were desperate for immediate income which did not allow them the luxury of waiting until a clientèle could be developed over time. They worked wherever they could. A few of the 20 have since passed away.

THUAN LE

Thuan now looks back on a career of over 30 years as an entrepreneur and pioneer in manicuring and nail art. As an independent contractor, she is self-employed and maintains her own schedule. She rents a booth at the same Brentwood area beauty shop in Santa Monica where she started her career. Even when her clients move away to Beverly Hills or further they come back to her. When people ask why she did not own a nail salon she says, "Everyone is not the same. Every success requires a lot of energy. We all have different needs and wants. I did not want my own nail salon. I just needed to work, have time to raise my children when they were young and to be happy with my family. I am a success in my own way."

Although, the salon has changed locations three times over the years, Thuan has developed and maintains deep relationships with her long-time customers. "I love my customers as friends, as family members." She has shared weddings and Bar Mitzvahs with them and has been intertwined in their lives.

When her children grew up and went to college, Thuan went back to school. She gained new licenses as a cranial and facial mas-sage therapist. She is also a Reiki Master. Reiki is the Japanese technique for stress reduction. She uses these skills to help herself, her clients and her family when needed. Now, the mani-curist and her friends are growing old together. Her children and their children have grown to adulthood. Thuan's children have all graduated from college and chosen careers. None chose manicur-ing. She and Trang have four grandchildren.

From left. Thuan Le, Tippi Hedren and actress,
Kieu Chinh 2013. Courtesy of NAILS MAGAZINE

When she looks back, she is profoundly happy with her life. She always recounts how Tippi Hedren is a lady with a kind heart for people and animals. "She lifted me up during the darkest time of my life with her love. She gave us love and courage and showed us the vision. She helped us to start a new life in a new country. That love started in 1975 at Hope Village. Tippi continues to reach out and change the lives of people for the better. That love has been painting the world with multi- colors!"

Yen Rist 2014

YEN RIST

At age 65, Yen has her own business providing permanent makeup called "Permanent Makeup by Yen Rist." Her business is located in a rental space inside the biggest beauty salon in her area called J. Russell Salon and Spa. She focuses on hair styling and permanent makeup services. She is glad that the days of frantic "survival" are over. She leads a very comfortable life now. "I deserve it, and I am relaxed." She is divorced with two sons and a daughter. None of her children pursued manicuring as a career.

Yen adds, "Without Tippi, there would be no nail industry as it is today!" She was the one to inspire the original manicurists like Thuan Le to succeed. She inspired those who came later and didn't speak English. There was no advantage to her. Tippi did it all with her heart, her love."

Becky and Charles Hambelton 2014

BECKY AND CHARLES HAMBELTON

Becky and Charles Hambelton still own the Citrus Heights Beauty College today. They owned the college the day that actress Tippi Hedren came in to talk with them about enrolling 20 Vietnamese women in a manicuring course. Becky was asked why they chose to help the refugee women back in 1975. "I felt they needed a chance." The couple is delighted at the success of their former students and the impact that manicuring has had in the lives of Vietnamese women." Becky continues, "We as a college felt very proud that we could help them with their lives. Our other students were inspired by their sacrifice, hard work and dedication to learn-ing the profession. The definition of success is helping others to succeed."

Charles Hambelton is now retired. Becky Hambelton currently manages the beauty college. Their son and daughter followed them into the field of cosmetology.

Minh and Kien Nguyen, founders of Advance Beauty College

MINH AND KIEN NGUYEN

Minh and Kien Nguyen took their inspiration from their friend Thuan Le, one of the first 20 manicurists in the United States. They made history by founding and operating the first Vietnamese beauty college, Advance Beauty College in Garden Grove, California. In 2011, it received the California Small Business of the Year award.

They are now both retired.

Minh and Kien passed Advance Beauty College on to their children, Tam and Linh Nguyen. The Nguyens are like most families, as parents they want their children to have a better life than they had. Consequently, the first generation's goal was to pave the way so their children had better options. Kien is happy that her children now operate the beauty college. She explains that, "They manage it the modern American way. The students, the teachers and the staff all report to the Director rather than the owners like in the old way. I'm very proud of them." Kien also notes that many former students have returned to share stories of their successes and she is pleased.

From left. Sen. Lou Correa presents Linh Nguyen,
Dr. Tam Nguyen and their father Minh Nguyen with the
California "Small Business of the Year 2011" award.
It's a family affair!

Thuan Le pictured with Dr. Tam Nguyen and Linh Nguyen,
current owners of Advance Beauty College.
Courtesy of NAILS MAGAZINE

Dr. Tam Nguyen, President, Advance Beauty College

Dr. Tam Nguyen *1.5 Generation*

Tam Nguyen and his sister Linh co-own Advance Beauty College in Orange County California's "Little Saigon," the mecca of Vietnamese-American culture. Tam was born in Vietnam and immigrated after the Fall of Saigon in 1975 with his parents, Minh and Kien Nguyen. At the time he was a babe in arms just 1½ years old and his mother was pregnant with his sister who was born months later in the United States. As Tam explains it, "This means that my father is 1st generation. I am 1.5 generation being born in Vietnam, which qualifies me as a refugee, but raised to adulthood in the United States." Tam's sister is 2nd generation having been born and raised in the United States.

Growing up, Tam's parents largely sheltered him from their traumatic experiences in war-torn Vietnam and their subsequent escape ordeal. When asked, they shared bits and pieces of their war experiences with him. Their focus was not on the past but on assimilating as quickly as possible and working hard to provide for their family. The Nguyens named their first business the "Tam Beauty Salon" after their son.

Tam's parents had a master plan. Tam would become a medical doctor and their daughter would manage the beauty college. It would be the fulfillment of their American dream. The plan was working out great through Tam's undergraduate years while his sister was working on a degree in business. His parent's hopes and dreams were still on course when Tam graduated from medi-cal school. Without notice, the master plan was suddenly derailed.

"I had been a good son, an obedient son who did everything my parents desired," Tam said. "I respected my Mom and Dad for coming to America with just the shirts on their backs. They were willing to work hard to give us the best life they possibly could."

Despite his appreciation, Tam had a dream of his own.

Through his education he had learned that in America, "the land of opportunity, you follow your heart, your passion and do what makes you happy." Tam had an internal conflict. Should he become a doctor, maybe a very unhappy doctor, just to make his parents happy or should he be really happy in a career which he loved and where he could still make a positive impact on society? Education he felt was just as important as medicine. Through education he could touch many people and not just one patient at a time.

The clash and climax came on medical school graduation day.
Tam put his foot down, he rebelled and resisted for the first time in his life. "I remember holding my degree and crying when I handed my M.D. degree to my Dad. I said Dad, 'This is for you.'" I told him then that I wanted to get a Master's Degree in Business and work in the family business, the beauty college. My Mom was very un-happy and against my choice. She had hoped to have her dreams realized when I finished a residency and started a practice as a doctor. She thought it was going to be a slam dunk!

My Dad surprised me. He said, "Son, I've come to realize that being in America it is important for you to be happy, and if you are happy we will be happy too." That conversation took place 14 years ago in 2000. It was the turning point in Tam's life. With their support, Tam completed his education at U.C. Irvine and Cal State Fullerton.

Today, Tam is not just happy about his career choice; he is ec-static about it. He loves managing Advance Beauty College with his sister. Over the years Advance Beauty College specializing in manicuring has graduated more than 36,000 students from its two campuses. One thousand students graduate annually and 450 are usually enrolled at any given time. The schools' continued success has given Tam the opportunity to give back to his community by serving on numerous committees and boards. For example, Tam leads the Diversity Task Force of the prestigious American Association of Cosmetology Schools. The American Association of Cosmetology Schools was founded in 1924. It represents thousands of beauty colleges nation-wide with regard to beauty, wellness and advocacy. Tam is the first Asian to serve on its Board of Directors. In addition, Dr. Nguyen has served as a consultant in Vietnam, his birthplace. He is married with 3 small children.

Linh Nguyen, Director, Advance Beauty College

LINH NGUYEN Second *Generation*

Linh Nguyen co-owns Advance Beauty College with her brother Tam. She is the Director. The college has two campuses, one in Garden Grove and one in Laguna Hills, California. Linh was born in California and graduated from the University of California, Fullerton with a degree in business. She had a cosmetology instructor's license at the age of 19. This allowed her to help in the family business and gain valuable experience early.

Linh looks to the growth, expansion and diversity of the future of their beauty college. The co-owners focus their efforts on us-ing the best in new products and technology. They also serve the community. Diversity is one of the school's key goals. They serve Cambodian, Korean, Japanese and students from all races and ethnicities. Written materials are in English and Vietnamese. They have a Russian teacher. They welcome new immigrants who have English as a second language. Their goal, Linh says, "is to de-velop well-rounded workers who are educated in *local* customs." As a subject-matter expert Linh is sought to review written and practical state licensing test materials for the Board of Barbering and Cosmetology. She is also active with the *National-Interstate Council of State Boards of Cosmetology*. Linh is currently pursuing a Master's Degree in Business Administration. Linh is married with 3 small children.

Advance Beauty College, Garden Grove, California

Chapter 8

CUSTOMER RANTS, RAVES AND REVIEWS

The Internet and Social Media provide customers a way to express their feelings about services they receive. Customers have a lot to say about nail salons. Here they share their candid unvarnished opinions. Comments are otherwise not edited. The comments are good, bad and ugly. The views expressed are not those of the author.

RAVE

L. S.

You know you're in Los Angeles when your neighbor on the soft, pillowy banquette at the corner nail salon is a dog. But even a small terrier yapping beside us couldn't throw our focused techni-cian off her game. She expertly exfoliated, buffed, and sculpted before delivering a massage. We walked away 30 minutes later with bone-dry nails—and not a smudge in sight.

RAVE

G.G.

You don't come to the Four Seasons Spa for cutting-edge polish colors or wacky lacquers. You come to drop a shoe size. At the newly opened luxurious facility, ____, who's been manicuring celebrities (like Juliette Binoche and James King) for 25 years rubs, files, and exfoliates haggard cuticles and the thickest of cal-luses until they disappear. When the smoke clears, you'll have the hands and feet of a newborn. The vigorous postoperative rubdown is fabulous, but your feet will be tender for a day or two.

RAVE

Melissa W.

I love this place! I always find the right time to come when it is not too busy. I have had Yvonne and Kathy do my nails, and love them. They do a great job with gel nails, and relaxing and efficient pedicures. Very clean, and nice staff.

RAVE

Los Angeles

P.W.

I got a Groupon for my fiancé for Hammer & Nails, which I was a bit nervous about because he's never been to a pampering type place, not even to get a haircut, since he's straight up bald. Not being the metro type, he wasn't exactly excited about the gift. Naturally, I forced him into going on the condition that I go with him. When we arrived I walked him in and got him all set up. The place was empty except for one other guy who seemed to be enjoying himself. When I went to sit down I was literally told to leave. I guess it's really a guy's thing only. I was a bit put off that she kind of forced me out and in a not so nice tone, but I overlooked it and left to my fiancés initial dismay. I got a few texts like, 'ugh you said you would wait for me! I hate you!'

I had no problem leaving, clearly I'd rather be window shopping than watch a man get his toe nails clipped, let's get real. Anyway, we met up afterwards and I was expecting a full on 'I'M NEVER DOING THAT AGAIN!" BUT, he was pleasantly surprised and I wouldn't be surprised if he starts making regular appointments, which he should- awe my little boy is growing up! He said the women was super friendly and offered him a drink and to watch whatever he wanted on TV, but they wound up just chatting instead. He said it felt amazing- duh, why do you think girls are smarter and do this on the regular. He also met the owner who was very kind as well, and he left quite happy and proud of his newly buffed toes and fingers. "She said I have nice feet," he bragged. "I bet she tells that to all the guys..." Overall, it's a great place to get your man or yourself some nail treatment, especially for those manly men who need to make baby steps into the metro male side.

INTERNATIONAL

Glitterati

Bangkok,

Thailand N.N.N.

Impressed with the variety of products they have here. Latest collections from many good brands like OPI, Shellac, Chanel, Essie, Zoya etc. I also like the fact that they carry the SpaRitual brand as well, I need the organic nail lacquer from time to time just to keep my nails in a good condition. Reasonable price. Very nice and well trained staff! Highly recommended.

RAVE

J.N.C.

This Sunset Plaza salon employs "nail cultivists" schooled in an all-natural system. Appointments take an hour, which may be why these manicures last. And where else can you see regulars Nancy Reagan (with her Secret Service agent), Jodie Foster, and Gina G. After a hangnail and cuticle cleanup, our manicurist filed our nails and massaged our hands with cream before slipping them into thermal mittens. Another staffer soaked our feet in a menthol-chamomile bath, trimmed our toenails with an angled clipper, exfoliated our skin with an almond-scented scrub, and massaged our feet and calves. We understood why so many women have had standing appointments here for 25 years.

RAVE

Rhonda, Los Angeles

I was thoroughly impressed by IBIZA Nail & Spa Services. Called and made last minute appointment for a friend and I, and was instantly taken care of when we walked in the door. We each got the Divine Mani & Pedi (Gel Mani), and so we had two people working on each of us simultaneously. Both the gentlemen who were working on me were friendly, and when it got to the part of the pedicure that always tickles the crap out of me, the guy took it easy so it wasn't unbearable. They had a huge assortment of colors and designs, which was awesome. Some places have limited options to choose from, but that was not the case here!! I definitely was a bit worried walking up that it wasn't going to be a clean place, but it was! I was thoroughly surprised. My nails have held up quite well so far, both on my gel Mani and my Pedi, and that's with traveling since I got it done.

RAVE

Justin W.

My wife made me clean up my nails, so I went downstairs to _____ Nail and asked for a manicure. I assumed that it was a place for women, but it turned out to be very comfortable for men. Thanks honey!

RANT

Shelia M.

Been there on my last visit to CA. If you are looking for a quick fix you MAY consider this place, otherwise stay away if you are look-ing for a relaxing/pampering experience. They rush you out those chairs, as if there is a race. The massage of my hands and arms were super hard, I had to remind her couple of times that she is hurting me. If hygiene matters to you (The towels were super dirty and disgusting, my towels fell couple of times and she kept using them with all the dust and hair it collected from the floor). I'm not going there again.

RAVE

Carla C.

Have been going there for the past 6 years or so but was getting tired of the long waits, even with an appointment have had to wait up to 40 minutes and they were almost always uncomfortably packed so decided to give Ibiza Nails a try as it is within my area and seemed nice. Got a full set of pink and white by Michelle and a gel pedicure by another technician and both were perfect. The shop itself is much more airy and even when there are lots of people it is spaciously designed and QUIET compared to the an-noying noisiness that's always at my old place. Parking was avail-able in their lot which is great as I used to have to pay $4 to park.
Will definitely be returning again.

RANT

Cora B.

Very mediocre place for a simple Mani ($12). The work was a bit sloppy (i.e. nail polish on my fingers) and they never dried it prop-erly so the moment I reached into my purse to get my keys BAM two nails ruined. I'm pretty annoyed but whatever I guess I'll just find another place.

RAVE

Elizabeth L.

Had my nails done here this afternoon and I enjoyed the experi-ence. I had a full set done and the lady working on them (did not catch her name) was super sweet and she took her time. I've avoided acrylics in the past because I hate sitting still for long periods of time and I really hate the smell of the acrylics, but I'm starting an internship Monday and wanted them to look nice. However, I found this place was airy enough and it didn't bother me. The only reason I'm giving 4 stars instead of 5 is because my cuticles are a bit beat up after she finished. I will definitely return. It's also close to my house which is a plus!

RANT

Ali H.

I went in for a gel manicure. I sat down and the woman proceeds to take my gel polish off. I knew right off the bat she wasn't experienced. She barely put any acetone on my nails. She had all 10 of my fingers in foil for over 15 minutes and every time she attempted to scrap the gel off it wasn't soaked enough for it to peel off. Finally I said to the woman who barely spoke 2 words of English that I wanted someone else who had experience taking off gel polish. (This was now 20 minutes and my poor fingers were still wrapped with foil) by this point I was getting very irritated. The manager came and took over where the other one left off. I'm shocked that she was so rude to me considering she's the manager!! She didn't greet me or even acknowledge me. I felt like I was a murderer on trial. She had this soar face as she was doing my nails. HELLO- this is your JOB!!!! And I'm going to pay for this service. SMH Anyway she basically tells me the reason the gel isn't coming off is because the color is too dark. I'm thinking no. I've never had a problem removing my polish before? Besides, why even say that?! Isn't the customer always right? She was buffing my nails so hard they were starting to hurt. I just let her finish and I told her I don't want to continue with my manicure. She didn't say a word, she got up and handed the ticket. The owner was also there. He witnessed the entire incident but he didn't say a word either!!!! He was such an ass. I paid my bill and left. Went to some random place and had them finish my manicure. Totally an-noyed the shit out of me though. Very unprofessional. I will never ever go back there!

INTERNATIONAL

Toronto,

Canada Stevey

M.

I am particular about waxing, and do not normally expect to give out a full 5 stars, but I was happily proven wrong! Looking for a place for a quick upper lip wax on Yelp, Four Seasons had some great reviews so I headed on up there today. Walking in midday on a weekday I had no wait (nor did the woman walking in for a manicure in front of me). I was really amazed at just how clean this place actually is! Seriously, I wish I could get my home to shine like that... It's also a really cute decor, doesn't look like a typical nail salon (usually they seem very late 80s to me, lots of peach/pink/aqua and floral patterns), very modern but comfy. Lip wax was great despite being less than $10 with tax. I have sensitive skin, but she was thorough and it was a rare occasion when I did not walk out with my skin irritated (declaring "I HAVE HAD A

LIP WAX!!!" in bold deep red and itching/burning like crazy while I try to have some self-restraint and not rub it). Wax temperature was good, and technique was proper. I will confidently take more delicate parts of me back here, having used my lip as a guinea pig. Everyone was very polite but efficient. All around, really impressed, and I will happily continue visiting Four Seasons Nail & Spa for waxing, and am excited to try it out when I have an event warranting a once-a-year (for me) manicure/pedicure.

RAVE

Catherine

Went here from Yelp and I am impressed. I just got gorgeous, long tips put on with gel to adhere them. Kathy did an amazing job! She was very careful not to hurt my nails and cuticles. It was a special treat, a bit more than a Mani/Pedi but so much detail and work, I see why. I now have gorgeous, sexy, long nails! I will be back and I will see Kathy again!

RANT

Danielle D.

Well the place is clean & pretty but my 2 stars goes for the new owner guy... He stands at the front desk staring at you while the girls are BUSY doing your nails. He yells to the girls working which pedicure chair they need to go next while still working on you...

The energy is pretty mad makes you feel very rushed & totally un-relaxed... &&&& to top it off my pedicure was so not good I could totally tell that she was not very experienced..... This is my second time leaving there unhappy with my pedicures. Also the front desk guy does not keep your appt. time & forgets what you booked yourself for. So the whole time he's going over asking a bunch of questions. He's annoying!!!! && to top it all off he was standing there && walking around SMOKING an E cigarette!!!!!!!!! I won't be going back there.

RANT

Brenna G.

If you check-in on Yelp for your first time, you get a free 5-minute massage. It's just too bad that when you ask, they're going to act like they're doing you a favor and avoid doing it. Seriously. When I asked about the coupon, one of the manicurists ROLLED HER EYES and said she would get someone to do it. 15 minutes later, no one comes, so I ask the receptionist man for help--since he was walking around checking if everyone was happy. He tells me that all the manicurists had just left, and I was like WHAT? I just asked 15 minutes ago, and they (begrudgingly) said OK. He finally gets me someone else...and I kid you not, he says, "You better give us a good review on Yelp." I'm sure he meant it lightheartedly, but I didn't really appreciate that. The guy who gave me the massage though...he was awesome. It's been a couple months since my visit, but I think his name was Kenny. Or Eddie. I don't remember, but I liked him. Anyways, the place itself looks great, and it's super Hollywood. I came in with two other friends, who were satisfied with their Mani-Pedi. It was just unfortunate that I didn't have such a great time. I got a gel manicure and a regular Pedi ($60)...the women who did my nails rushed through it. When I turned around to check on my friends, they were only halfway through by the time I was finished and they didn't even get gel... I don't mind paying for quality and service, but from this experience I had neither. After only a few days, my gel manicure started cracking! I sent a picture over to my friend who owns a nail salon in Boston, and she said that whoever did it "sucks." The only reason why I'm giving this place three stars instead of two is because I really liked Kenny/Eddie who gave me my 5-minute massage. Please don't offer a coupon if no one who works there wants to actually do it. I don't expect people to kiss up to me when I get my nails done, but at the same time, I also don't want to be around employees who clearly hate their job. It reflects poorly on the salon.

RAVE

Liz

Clean, friendly, updated chairs. Great pedicure. Very good prices. Parking could be better, but where couldn't it be? This is going to be my go to nail salon in West Hollywood. Would LOVE it if they would change the video selections. An hour of Pink was just too much. We will see what they play next time!

RAVE

Jessie

First off, let me start by saying that I live in Santa Monica, and it sometimes takes upwards of an hour to get there. But, Liz is totally worth it. She takes her time and never rushes, which is a problem that I've had at many salons. Liz always exceeds expectations. I've had her do two designs on my nails, and each time I'm amazed that she can just look at the photo and know how to do it. I almost always make my appointments in advance with her because her appointments fill up quickly! It's also an extremely clean nail sa-lon with fair prices - $12 for a manicure and $25 for a pedicure. Coming from Santa Monica where the best regular manicure I got was $20, this is significantly better. My regular manicures also typically last about 1 1/2 weeks to 2 weeks, which is amazing. The only thing to think about when coming here is the parking. They have an extremely small parking lot, but there is plenty of free parking on N. Gardner Street.

RANT

l. A.

I bought my boyfriend a Mani/Pedi for Valentine's Day and he was so excited to redeem it but insisted that I accompany him. I wasn't going to get a service but figured I would come and watch. We didn't have an appointment but I figured it was okay since when I came in to buy the gift card on a Saturday afternoon it was completely empty. We walked in and like I figured, it was totally empty and when the woman at the front asked if he had an appointment, we said no and she seemed flustered. She told us to hold on and went to the back and came out again and answered the phone and then went back again to a back office. She finally told him to sit in one of the many empty chairs and I walked over with him. I asked where the restroom was and she said that someone was in it but for safety reasons, I have to sit in the front and wait. After using the restroom I sat in the chair next to my boyfriend and was told that the chairs were only for customers and I said can I sit next to him and if a customer needs it, I would get up. Let me remind you the place was totally empty! She said no and I got up to sit in the front. Then another woman comes up to me and says "let me explain to you our rules. Chairs are only for paying custom-ers." I said and when your employee told me to get up, I did and she responded well I was told you ignored her. I said to be honest, I'm not impressed with your customer service and feel accosted. I couldn't believe I was not allowed to sit with my boyfriend and now to have someone unnecessarily come over to "enforce their rules" is so rude. I will not be coming back. I love shark tank and saw the owner on it and he seemed so friendly and yet the staff here is so rude and unwelcoming, I would never recommend this place to anyone.

INTERNATIONAL

The Nail Studio
Lagos, Nigeria

As a pioneer in the African nail industry we are pleased to offer you a large range of nail services. We offer specialist manicures, pedicures and nail extension services which include acrylic, fiberglass and gel nails.

RAVE

Helena G., N. Carolina

I made an appointment a few weeks prior to my visit. I am the maid of honor for my sister's wedding. I made the appointment for 10 girls getting Mani/Pedi's or one or the other. I was afraid they would not have things organized and we had a whole day planned for our Bachelorette Day!!! We had a lunch reservation at

12:30 at the nearby Mediterranean restaurant. When we arrived they were ready for us right when they opened. There were practically 2 people per girl in case each and every one of us wanted both the Mani/Pedi. The women and men that did our nails were very detail and did not rush at their job. They did a wonderful job with everything and they even gave us coffee, chips, candy, and water during our visit with no extra charge! I love this salon and will definitely be back to when I am in the area! Thank you everyone!!!

RANT

Sharon

I made a manicure appointment a week in advance because I had a particularly busy schedule that day. When I got there the manager informed me that my appointment was actually at 11:15 rather than 11:00. I asked why nobody called me to let me know the change in time and she just brushed me off. After patiently waiting till 11:20, again, I asked the manager what happened and informed her that if someone doesn't start working on my nails now, I will be late for my next appointment. She begrudgingly said that she could start on my nails. Needless to say, I was late for my next appt.

RANT

Reported by WSB TV

It's normal practice for nail salons to charge for extra designs and services, but what about extra weight? The Georgia woman received a startling surprise after receiving a manicure, pedicure and eyebrow arch. The owner tacked on an extra $5 dollars to her bill for being overweight. Salon manager Kim explained that the extra fee was meant to cover the cost of replacing the $2,500 salon chair, in case it broke. I said, ", you can't charge me $5 more. That's discrimination because of my weight," the woman told WSB TV.

According to the salon owner, the chairs are meant to withstand only 200 pounds and anything above that weight could damage the chairs. "Do you think that's fair when we take $24 [for manicure and pedicure] and we have to pay $2,500? Is that fair?"

"No," said Kim in her defense. Kim has since refunded the woman $5 and told her to take her business elsewhere.

The woman, who was close to tears when given the news, would like more customers to learn about the salon's unfair practices. "The word has to get out there that these people are discriminating against us because of our weight," she said. "I mean come on, we're in America. You can't do that."

RANT

M.V., Kent, Washington

"This place provides such inconsistent service. When it is good, they knock it out of the park and when it is bad it is so awful. The massage is never good twice in a row; the massage sometimes is a barely touch with lotion and other times amazing with even a neck massage. You literally never know what you are in for, which makes it embarrassing when you invite people to go with you. Also even with an appt. you sometimes wait 1 min other times 35 minutes so yeah Good and bad. Prices are comparable to other places."

RAVE

T.B.G.

"I went into an Asian salon with my kids. I thought they gave me a kind of weird look at first. Made me think that it was for Asians only. But how hard can it be to use clippers and cut a boy's hair? The three girls there were really nice. They spoke to each other in Vietnamese, which made me feel like they were whispering in front of me. So, I just smiled. After they finished I offered my debit card for payment. They didn't have the set-up for it. Guess what? They let me write a check. I was very surprised, maybe they thought the potential of a bad check or any check would be better than no payment at all. My options were to go and get cash (and possibly never return) or to simply not pay. I just didn't expect they would take a check. All the other Asian businesses I've ever gone to won't take checks. I'll go back there again for my kids' haircuts and my brow waxing."

INTERNATIONAL

Loganc7, Berlin, Germany

"So, I went to Paradise Nails in the Wilmersdorfer Arcaden today for a pedicure and it was OK. I can't say it was fantastic, but I do think that they're really more set up for manicures. They did a fairly decent job, but I think I'm spoiled by the amazingly fantastic place I used to go to in New York! Paradise Nails seems to be a pretty standard shopping mall nail salon, though, and they look like they do everything - gel, acrylic, fancy designs, airbrushing, etc. Since I just had the pedicure, I can't really comment personally on the manicure services, but I'd say it's worth a shot!"

RANT

MD Mack

They moved and want to charge more for services. I asked why they went up they said you see all this we have to pay for this. To top it off when you get pedicures they put trash bags in the foot basin so they don't have to clean up after each use.

RAVE

Tim. M.

My wife goes here and I have on occasion been wrestled onto the white sofa-like bench while I soaked my toes. It's very clean, the ladies are nice and they have water. I really am picky about water, I know it's weird, but there's tasted like spring water. I can't say much since I'm a guy but I love the way my wife's nails and toes look after we leave this place. Parking sucks - go for the Valet.

RANT

G.U., Atlanta

I had a pedicure and was very excited to finally try this place. We were the last appointment of the day which they constantly kept reminding us of. They kept talking about how it was a long day and they finally get to go home. They rushed through, the water was cold, and the staff tried to act snooty and were super rude!!!! Never ever will I go back for what it costs!!!!!!!!!!!!

RAVE

W. Los Angeles, CA

We know change is good—but when our aesthetician tried to coax us from our square nails to rounder ones, we balked. But she promised that smoother edges would help stave off nail cracks and tears, so we yielded to her file. She rewarded us with a sooth-ing, hot-cream cuticle treatment and an arm-and-hand massage with Bliss's signature lemon-and-sage-scented lotion. And the change was well worth it—we haven't had a split nail since.

RAVE

N. G.

We don't live in Beverly Hills (except in our dreams), but we felt right at home there after a visit to this family-operated salon. N. entertained us with friendly repartee while she sculpted our nails to perfection. We enjoyed our conversation so much that we decided to prolong it by staying for a pedicure. Before we left, we promised to return soon—but our polish hasn't chipped once in two weeks. At this rate, we might start to get homesick.

INTERNATIONAL

Koco Nail Bar, Notting Hill, London

Koco Nail Bar is an ideal destination for frazzled parents. The nail bar itself is spacious and sleek with plenty of room for buggies and prams. But what really makes them special is their trained nanny, who is on hand every Tuesday to take care of your little ones, while you can relax with a cocktail or glass of champagne. The Signature Coco Manicure incorporates a standard manicure

together with a relaxing paraffin wax with essential oils. My finger-tips were wrapped in plastic and encased in soothing hot mitts
– utter heaven.

RAVE

M. M.

For a place that attracts such a highbrow clientele, Jessica's is decidedly low-key. There are no personal televisions, plush chairs, or rose petals floating in the footbaths—just meticulous groom-ing. Our manicurist began by filing our nails, pausing every few minutes to measure each tip against the others. Next, she gently pushed back our cuticles with a cool vibrating tool. The service might not have included any bells or whistles, but our glossy red polish got plenty of attention on its own.

RAVE

R.E.

"_____" is a real manicure visionary. Her nail spa ____ is known for its non-toxic ingredients, but her more extreme manicures for Lady Gaga and Fergie have included staples and nails (ouch!). For those of you who want a tamer ten, be sure you get one of her signature metallic Minx treatments: She swears the silver, gold, and chrome tones can't be mimicked with polish or airbrushing, and they're shiny enough to reflect light from a block away or in a dark nightclub.

RAVE

Ann, Y., Los Angles, California

"I just got back from my 1st visit to Nancy. She's THE ONE I've been searching for! A manicurist in a comfy salon, who isn't located too far, someone with skills, pays attention to detail, gentle, and approachable! I came in with a need to try out a different shape and she accommodated. She gave me great advice and I felt I could trust her. She'll chat with you, but when you're focused on reading a magazine or occupied with your phone, she'll continue doing her work. And I absolutely adore how she'll consistently check up with you if you are liking what she's doing. Her service is beyond any other Beverly Hills nail bar, no need to book a month in advance or pay triple the price for a quality set of nails! As for my pedicure.

Jenny did that and she is hands down the best pedicurist I've ever had. Oh my god that foot massage! And such detailing to her work as well. I've never had my toes nail beds cut before!!! Such a sweet lady and I love how she listens to me and makes my water super-hot. Just the way I like it! I'm definitely returning for my next fill and Pedi in two weeks."

RANT

Nancy, A., Florida

A Volusia County woman was arrested after several 911 calls to complain about a bad manicure.

On Sunday C. C., 44, from Deltona, was fighting with her nail technician at _____ Nails because she apparently didn't like the length of her nails. The woman was arrested for calling 911 to complain about the manicure. During the fight the nail technician was slightly injured but it was C. C. who called Volusia County Sheriffs deputies to the salon.

RAVE

Ruth C., Sacramento, California

"This is the only salon I will go to in Sacramento for a pedicure, and Kimmie is the very best! She always puts the comfort and desires of her clients first and is very gracious. You more than get your money's worth and Kimmie will go out of her way to make sure your feet feel great and your toes have the color you want, even taking the time once to have me come back for polish the next day so she could shop for the color I wanted in between my Pedi and the polish. Of course, you can bring in the color you want and save the trouble, but that's the level of customer service of-fered at Papillon! I first found Kimmie and most of the Papillon crew at a different salon further from my home, but when they came to Papillon, I followed and it's because they are that good! I am just lucky it's closer to my home in Natomas. This is not a rush you through $15 Pedi, or an okay $45 Pedi. It is a great mid-priced Pedi that usually takes 1.5 hours and leaves you feeling pampered and relaxed. I cannot recommend Kimmie highly enough so if you are looking for a Pedi to pamper you and make your toes look great, look no further, you have found the place! One final note, they carry OPI color selections my fave!"

INTERNATIONAL

Nail Bar – Beaute'
Dupin Paris France
Kathy N. of Sunshine Coast, Australia

Aussie just arrived in Paris in desperate need of manicure (gel) and Pedi. Made appointment, arrived 10 minutes later. Despite language barrier we managed to figure out what we were saying then her husband came in the door who spoke English and we had a fantastic three-way conversation. Nails look fab. Would go again if I return to Paris.

RAVE

R.M. Seattle, Washington

"This place is everything they say it is and more. They had all the nifty nail extras I wanted like glitter tips and extra pretty polishes. They were kind and I never once felt rushed like I do in most salons. I will be back as soon as possible for my next Mani/Pedi!"

RAVE

Charise L. Renton, Washington

"Been going here for years! Hong is great and always does what I want and I'm super picky!"

RANT

Keke L. Austin, Texas

"The owner does the best eyebrows in Austin; however, her atti-tude is what made me stop going to the shop. That says a lot! First of all, 99.9% of the time when I wanted her to do my eyebrows she told me, 'No,' and to let one of the other girls do it. I would always say *No, I want you to do them.* It was always a constant battle with her. She was always rude! One time she told me I was pretty. The next time she told me I ugly. One day she said, 'See aren't you glad I done your eyebrows. Now you pretty. Before you ugly.' LOL I can laugh at it now, but when she made that comment, I was totally in shock and extremely pissed. I couldn't believe she had such cus-tomer service skills and was so disrespectful. I often wondered how her shop was still in business. Her shop deserves zero stars; however, that's not an option. She received two because she really does a great job doing eyebrows. Every time I went to her shop, I left feeling insulted. I was always saying to myself, *did she really say that?* And, *why do you still go to her?* The final straw: I asked her to do my eyebrows. The battle began, 'No, let the other girl do it.' Me: *No, I want you to do them.* Blah, blah, blah. Finally she says, 'Well you'll have to wait until I finish her eyelashes.' I said, *that's fine.* She finished the ladies eyelashes and sat down. I looked at her with a look of confusion. She looked at me and pointed to a lady who was currently receiving a pedicure and said, 'She's next.' I replied, *she's getting her toes done, can't you do my eyebrows in the meantime.* She said, 'No, I'll have to ask her' (referring the client). She asked the client was it ok and the lady said, 'Yes.' The owner tells me to go to the eyebrow seat. As I'm walking to the back, I hear the owner say, 'You need to tell her thank you. Um, ma'am you heard me, you need to tell her thank you.' I didn't know who she was talking to, but I stopped and looked back and she has her hand on her hip while pointing to the lady in the pedicure chair. 'Tell her thank you,' she said. I said, *Tell who thank you and why?* I was confused. She said, 'Her for letting you go before her.' My frustration and anger for this woman grew. I calmly turned my head without saying anything and went to the chair. As I walked to the seat, the owner said, 'Oh don't worry about her she's just ghetto.' Now I'm livid! Like really, WTH? Who acts like this? I maintained my composure because I really needed my eyebrows done! I didn't say a word. I was pissed! After that occurrence, I've never gone back. I've been strong. Obviously, the owner doesn't know how to interact with people in a professional manner. She's rude and full of insults. She's extremely ghetto and I will never give her my business again regardless of her talent(s)."

RAVE

K.K. Atlanta

S. has a convenient location right next to the new Buckhead Atlanta Mall along with a beautiful glamorous atmosphere and cozy lounge seating to relax on after a long day of shopping. This is where the real pampering begins.

RAVE

G. U., Atlanta

Really love this nail salon. Extremely, extremely clean and sanitary - which is a must for me. By far, the BEST place for a Shellac mani-cure in Atlanta. All of the technicians do a fantastic job on my nails and if by chance one them chips - I can stop by there before the 'two week guarantee' is up and they will fix it at no charge. Been to both Buckhead and Va Highlands locations. Buckhead one is a bit more cramped inside and I don't like having to valet my car, but the service there is still amazing! My only complaint would be get-ting pedicures. I am fine with passing on a hand massage and just getting the Express Mani, but I get a pedicure more for relaxation than anything else. The least expensive pedicure with a massage is $28 and I don't feel like I'm really getting my money's worth out of it. They rub my legs for less than 3 minutes every time and at that price I feel like that just isn't worth it for me. If I'm going to pay a bit more than other places I should at least get a 10-15 minute leg massage.

RANT

SMH.

OMG! Someone finally gets it. While some of these Asians are scrubbing your feet they are driving Lexus and having mansions while some of these people are complaining about their language barrier.

RAVE

S.O.

Beverly Hills is the first place we'd look for a top-notch nail salon—and the last place we'd expect to find a bargain. But that was before we visited this family-operated gem. N. neatened up our cuticles and filed away every ridge while T. simultaneously got to work on our feet, scrubbing away our calluses and treating us to a generous toe-to-knee massage. Both applied polish without a smudge and sent us on our way with pristine nails that remained chip-free for two weeks, exceeding our expectations— but not our budget.

RAVE

E.A.

In 2003, Es opened up in Tokyo, Japan, deriving their name from the initials of "elegant satisfaction." They brought their signature style of high-fashion Japanese 3D Nail art to LA in 2012, and ever since, there's been a line out the door. If you want rhinestones, studs, gradation, glitter, lace appliqués, or all of the above, the artists will find a way to make a version that fits your nails. Be warned though: when all is said is done, your manicure can run as high as $130.

RANT

B.F., New York

It is now a holiday weekend and I am graduating Tuesday, and left scrambling to find a salon that will fix this mess. Oh, and by the way, do NOT ask for nail art either (they have it on the price list). I asked her to do a simple V-shape French on the bottom, and it looked like a child drew it. Seriously, my boyfriend knows nothing about nails and even he noticed it looked "off".

INTERNATIONAL

Salt and Chocolate, Knightsbridge, Walton Street, England Chloe

There aren't many establishments where you can get your nails done and purchase an original, signed fashion print at the same time, but this is what Russian fashion writer and socialite Yana Uralskaya has created at Salt & Chocolate. I sat and admired the pictures by renowned photographers such as Terry O'Neill and Shlomi Nissim, while the quiet but meticulous therapist set to work. Opt for the Classic Manicure, which is pretty much the same as the Luxury Manicure, bar a homemade sugar and lavender scrub.

RAVE

M.E.

The manicures here are amazing. Unbelievable really. This is not the type of salon you come to for a pampering experience, where you get a massage, or that type of thing. This is the place you come to if you want to rock ridiculously intricate and beautiful gel designs for upwards of three weeks. My nails look awesome, I get compliments on them every day, and they've lasted forever without a chip.

RANT

Ella H.

I love the no chip policy here during a weekday. However, beware, if you call and make an appt. at busier times they will say "Yes, come in at 2" But it is not an appt. When you get there you will wait until there is an available manicurist. This has happened twice. 1st time I waited 20 minutes. The second time I waited 40 minutes and finally left. So if you need a specific appt. time, make that very clear.

RAVE

Emily A. Seattle, Washington

I have been back several times since my first review, and I'm still just as pleased. Each time I'm in I get a different one of the staff for my pedicure, but there is a consistency between techniques of the ladies there- which is really comforting since most salons vary so wildly between staff member's ability and technique. There's actually plenty of parking too, if you go to the right of the mini mart there's more spaces, I've been on some super busy days and never had to turn away or wait due to a lack of spots. And once more,

I'd really like to reiterate their color options! Soooo many choices, a huge variety of colors and sparkles.... And it's not just a variety of reds and pinks, but greens, purples, orange, blue...! Literally almost anything you could want. Their hygiene, esp. when treating a wound on a pedicure or acrylic nail set is in fact up to WA state code. I am a nationally licensed cosmetologist, and have seen a few incidents (they happen!! Feet are wound magnets sometimes) where the girls handled the wound professionally, and with every effort to keep the client comfortable. They obviously never intend for that to happen but in a nail salon it is just the way it is. If you're in pain or uncomfortable, tell your nail tech- they can help! It's their job! And the owner Hong is always there, speak to her!!! All in all, I still drive here every time I need a pedicure, all the way from Seattle. And even when I think of going to a closer place... I can't do it... They're so rad here, and I know I won't be able to match their ability at another salon. So I take the trek, for a...excuse me...

Damn fine pedicure. :)

RAVE

Cat T., Seattle, Washington

"I rarely go out to get manicures and pedicures. However, I will block off time to pamper myself whenever there's a special occasion coming up. So when a formal work dance was coming up on a Friday night, I asked for suggestions on where to get a mani-cure before the big event. I chose to go to _____ after work on a Thursday night for its convenience in location (I work in Renton) and high reviews. I didn't make an appointment, but let me tell you I definitely should have made one! I ended up waiting around 45 minutes before someone was free to take care of my mani-cure. It goes to show how popular this nail salon is. Thankfully, there were plenty of magazines to look at, so I got my gossip and style fix during the wait. I wish I caught my nail technician's name she did a great job on my nails! She shaped my nails very nicely, gave me a relaxing hand and forearm massage, and the nail pol-ish application was well done. PLUS, once she was done painting my nails, she got up and gave me an awesome neck and back massage. Sweet! Total cost for a manicure plus massage: $15 (before tip) the one con that comes to mind is the nail polish (non-Shellac) selection I wasn't very impressed. I'm the kind of girl who prefers soft pinks, wine reds and nudes, and I didn't see much of that in their selection. Rather, I saw a lot of bright, neon, metallic, and glitter colors I probably shouldn't be rockin' in the workplace (at least for manicures). This made choosing a nail polish color a little more difficult than expected. Plus, the nail polishes were a bit all over the place; I ended up walking back and forth between two shelves before striking gold with a Sephora by OPI pink nail polish. Not sure if their nail polish collection is large enough to warrant more organization, but it'd be nice to see the nail polishes organized according to shades, or maybe even by brand. Overall, I had a good experience at _____. Good service, high quality results and fair prices. My manicure still looked good after one week! I'd come back whenever I have a special occasion coming up, and I'll remember to make an appointment beforehand."

INTERNATIONAL

Nailbar AD, Italy

This modern new salon is, in fact, set up like a bar, with rows of brightly colored polish on the shelves below the alcoholic beverages. They pride themselves in treating clients to a New York-style manicure, with three to four coats of polish, careful attention paid to cuticles, and instruments sterilized with a state of the art system used by doctors and dentists. Also on offer are gels and fills, and pedicures, both aesthetic and curative, performed in the luxury of massage chairs. For the body, there is a sun shower, massages and peels. A menu of facial treatments are on offer, using the French Decleor line and the Lanèche range of products from Holland. Parties can be booked for a girl's night out, com-plete with real beverages at the bar, and for special occasions, a makeup artist is on call. Nailbar is the sole Italian retailer of American Nails products, which ironically, are manufactured in
Germany.

RANT

Carmen R. Vallejo, California

"The truth is *LOCATION IS EVERYTHING*! This nail shop is probably one of the best full service nails salons (nails, feet, waxing and lashes). But on the other hand the owner's ghetto mentality over-shadows the staff's skills. The services! She's disrespectful and thinks she's one of the gang. Asking about, 'Yo baby daddy' and 'why yo man ain't paying for you to get your nails done.' So if you don't mind being insulted and listening to ghetto slang mentality this is the shop for you!"

RANT

C.M., Seattle, Washington

"Came here with a friend who has gone here before. I like that the prices are reasonable, but it can get busy. The hardest part about coming here is the parking and the workers. While the workers are super sweet, clearly some are not fluent in English and it shows.
The woman who gave me my pedicure didn't understand that I wanted an Ultimate Pedicure. I ended up with a deluxe first world problem. I know. Then, she didn't understand that I wanted the mud mask and NOT the paraffin wax. Four chattering girls later, the mother hen--aka the Owner--stepped in and asked what I wanted--all in flawless English. The girl who did my toes was a bit clip happy with the nail cutters and I do have very sensitive toes. She cut them fairly close to the quick, which made me flinch. However, because the girl didn't speak English, it was hard to convey how uncomfortable I was feeling with her rapid clipping. Would I come here again? Maybe, but for now, I think I'll be hunting for a new place."

RANT

C.V., NJ

I understand this woman's point. My GF goes to a salon and she says that it's quite intimidating asking for a service when the staff of the salon don't speak English. Also if they're anything like what I have experienced they cut corners where ever they can. So they can be talking about you and giving you an infection without you even noticing. The Vietnamese are nice people, but if you give them an inch they will take a mile if they can.

RANT

Wendy D.

Had a Pedi-party here. Embarrassed that I even suggested it. The pedicures lasted 15 minutes for $28. Save your money and go somewhere that will spend at least the same amount of time as you pay for the pedicure.

RANT

GLORIA

I was thinking about booking a Mani/Pedi party at _____ the day before my upcoming wedding for all my bridesmaids, Mom, cousins, etc. I thought I would check it out with a friend first. I am glad I did. I called and made an appointment for 5:45 and told them we would try and get there but might be a little late. They said that was fine but that they would need a credit card to hold the appointments. I inquired about the cancellation policy and they told me 24 hours' notice or I would be charged. Working for a small business myself,

I understand that they can't hold spots and miss out on other cli-ents and then not get paid. So I gladly gave him my credit card information to hold our spots. We got there at 5:54pm. They told us that one of us could only have either a Mani or Pedi since we were late. So I offered to just take the manicure so my friend could get both services. They started my manicure while my friend sat and waited....and waited....and waited. It soon became clear they gave one of our appointments away to a walk-in customer so I asked to speak to the manager. I explained that I paid to hold the spots and did not understand why they had not even started the Mani/Pedi for my friend. (Not to mention that basic logic dictates if one person is getting a Mani/Pedi and the other person only a Mani; it is prob-ably best to start the Mani/Pedi first). He was the one I spoke with on the phone so I reminded him that I told him we might be running a little late and he said that was fine. At that point, he said they tried to call us but the line was busy. Not true since I have call waiting on my cell phone, which was the number I gave them. Further, there was no record of their "attempted call." The manager told me it was my fault for being late and that we must have had a misunderstand-ing. No apology. No attempt to fix the situation or offer to make other appointments. I was really dumbfounded since I told them I was thinking about booking a party with 8 deluxe Mani/Pedi's the day before my wedding. It was clear the people working there were dying to end their work day and were not willing to stay one extra minute overtime. I basically just paid $17 for half of a manicure at that point and we left and went somewhere else. Needless to say, I found another place to book my pre-wedding party. If someone is not willing to at least be polite to a customer who wants to book over $600 worth of services, I cannot bring myself to return. Not to mention that one of my cuticles is still bleeding today from my 1/2 manicure. Too bad because the place is cute and would have been perfect for the big group party I had in mind. What a bummer!

RAVE

T.S.

I love _____ Nails. They are always able to seat me for a Mani & Pedi without a delay. They have a great color selection. Inside the salon is very clean and the staff is friendly. They always offer you beer, wine or water. They have a great system that usually gets you in and out in a very timely manner. They usually do your Mani and Pedi at the same time, which I love! PS: The inside view shown on google is a little dated. They have added many more Pedi chairs along all three walls with the Mani stations in the middle. This works out really well and doesn't feel crowded at all. In response to a customer that said that you can't tell them you didn't like something, there have been plenty of times when I didn't like the color or perhaps it chipped a little after I left. I swung back by and they were more than happy to fix it for me!

RANT

G.U.

Do not state that you don't agree with their mistakes at this place. They will state that you are too picky! They are serving wine, and do not have a liquor license to do so as well. Also, I have been cut while having my manicure. HORRIBLE. By the way, they are not listed in the Better Business Bureau.

RAVE

R.

There's usually a wait at _____ so be sure to make an appointment in advance. Once inside, take a seat with Sam, the airbrush-ing artiste, who within minutes will have your paws painted in any style you like. Last time we got watermelon, but next we're asking Sam the Man to give us a swallow-print paint job à la Miu Miu's spring dresses!

INTERNATIONAL

Madrid,

Spain Debs.

M.

I was initially quite excited about visiting _____ as I'd heard good things from friends. However, my experience was lackluster. Although the manicurist herself was lovely and very nice to chat to, I felt rushed around and like the management were desperate to get me in and out as fast as they could, despite it not being all that busy at the time. The manicure itself chipped very quickly and for the price I paid, it definitely wasn't worth the experience.

RAVE

B.W.

My sister Tess and I went to this radical nail art salon called _____ on Melrose Ave. in Los Angeles to get our nails did. This Japanese owned and operated salon boasts the most skilled nail artists in the business, these girls are truly amazing!

I went **totally bonkers** and had them do every nail different with tie dye, glitter and giant Swarovski crystal gems and bows – I figured, why not!? My sister went for a more toned down **black and white** drips, polka dots and bows look... we love how they turned out! the price of $120 (for the most detailed nail art designs) makes manicures like these, best suited for special occasions, but the salon does offer a variety of pricing options and endless design possibilities!

They use gel polish for the color and acrylic medium to attach the 3D elements. The gems are stuck on so strong there is NO risk of them falling off – I've been bonking them all over the place and they've stayed strong and shiny! I'm going to try to interpret these techniques in my own DIY nail art!

RAVE

C.C.

We're ashamed to admit how bad it had gotten. Our calluses had calluses, and two of our fingernails were so split that Cianciotto, who has tended to Kelly Preston and Barbara Bush, had to pry off the Band-Aids before getting to work. She filed, scrubbed, and generally performed a beauty intervention on our fingernails until they were almost unrecognizable—in a good way. Then she moved on to our sorry feet. Cianciotto won't touch razors. Instead, she rubbed our soles with a dose of sloughing lotion made with olive pits and peppermint, and then worked her nail voodoo with a special buffer that abolishes all ridges. The finale, an intense reflexology massage, made us feel utterly and unspeakably serene.

RAVE

L.S., New York

Whoever said that bad things come in threes never stopped by this uptown salon for a simultaneous manicure, pedicure, and blowout. Our nail technician, steered us away from the dark brown shade we selected, suggesting a deep purple to suit our fair skin.

While she filed our toes, V. got to work on our blowout, smoothing out every kink. Next, S. moved on to our hands, giving our nails a squarish shape to go with our edgy polish. We left with gleaming fingers, toes, and hair—a true triple threat.

RAVE

J.S.

We never quite understood why hot milk makes people sleepy—until we ventured into Jin Soon. We soaked our hands in a bowl of warm milk, honey, and grapefruit essence, which felt so calming and hydrating that our manicurist practically had to pry out each hand for filing. When our nails were shaped to the ideal round-ness, she massaged a lemon-scented exfoliator up to our elbows, and rubbed our arms and hands again with a velvety moisturizer. After a wrap of steaming towels, she painted on a light pink shade. By the end, we were feeling smooth and ready for a nap.

RAVE

C.B.

The place: The big, open space looks nothing like a nail salon, with contemporary light fixtures and royal blue banquette seating, which allows you to sit and chat with a friend during a manicure.

What we asked for: After flipping through the salon's menu of 25 nail-art styles, we chose a mash-up of Weekend Update (rainbow confetti glitter tips) and Bling Ring (rhinestone appliqués with bare half-moons). **The extras:** Clients can take a slightly cheesy Mani-cam photo of their nails to share on social media. **Bottom line:**

_____ experimented with polish colors until we were happy with a peachy nude half-moon and graphite glitter tips. It cost more than we normally pay for simple nail art, but we did like being able to combine two designs from the menu, and the result was cooler than expected.

RANT

M.B.

Dirty smelly horrible service a bunch of women speaking a language back n forth you don't understand NOT relaxing at all!!!!! Go across town.

RAVE

Sharon K., Seattle

I live and work on the Eastside, so I've always gotten my nails done in my general area, and have never given up hope that I'd find a nail salon that I would love enough to make it my regular spot. I've come close a couple of times, but there's always been something that wasn't great enough to inspire loyalty on my part. I found myself wandering in Seattle with my main squeeze and his little guy last Saturday, and while they were otherwise engaged,

I searched for a nail spot just for a polish change on my fingers and Pedi on the toes. I have acrylic nails, and didn't think it was time for a fill. Pedicure was excellent, and the young woman who worked on my feet used a callous razor, which I truly needed, since I tend to walk around barefoot a lot. But when it was time for the manicure, I was lucky enough to be paired with Anh. She took one look at my nails and showed me that my nails needed a fill, since they were separating. She gave me a time approximation, since she knew I needed to meet up with the guys again soon She also asked me if I wanted a more natural look, and proceeded to actually rebuild the nail, and shaped it with the sander machine instead of literally clipping it with the nail clipper like my regular salon. This took longer, but was incredibly thorough, and the nails turned out GORGEOUS. Looks like total natural nails (except for the amazing purple I picked out). This one is worth driving over to Seattle for. Prices were certainly competitive, and parking was not a problem. Awesome!

RAVE

N.S.

This is definitely my new spot to go to. Thanks to Tammy. I had been scared to do acrylic for a while ever since this other nail salon had kept cutting me, but Tammy listened and she knew what she was doing. Even though it's a small place with lots of people even from the start of the morning, they get to you very quick. It's quick, but they do a great job with your nails and take their time. It's in a nice place on lower Queen Anne by the Metropolitan. I know I'm not the only one who thinks the ladies at the nail salon are talking bad about the customers in their language, and I HATE that, BUT.... the girls here engage with you and they talk to you which is nice, instead of them screaming across the room, so it's a good vibe here. I really like that I've finally found a place that doesn't talk a bunch of crap. Will be coming here for all my nail appointments now :)

RAVE

W.W.

So excited to have found this place!! Just moved to Seattle a year ago and have tried at least ten different places and not super impressed. Was in search for someone who could take me as a last minute walk in on a Monday evening. My nails look amazing and it is literally the first time ever they have stayed on over a week without lifting! I am so excited!! I have the worst luck with gel/acrylic/shellac always lifting after a couple of days and then I just pick it all off -- ultimately unhappy that I spent the money on nails that last a week. This Monday is two weeks and they still look amazing! Great work, super quick and great prices!!

RAVE

C.D.

Okay, I'm going to be honest. I was originally going to the nail place just a few blocks away. But I guess they are closed on Tuesdays so back I went to try Top Nails. When I walked in, there were 3 people being worked on but I got seated at a Pedi station right away. Within 15 minutes, I was completely alone in the salon and had one lady (an older lady) working on my toes and one lady doing my nails.

The lady doing my toes WENT TO TOWWWN! I seriously don't think my feet have ever looked this good. She worked at them for so long and made sure they were perfectly smooth. The woman doing my nails gave me the longest hand massage I've ever had but that was probably because I was the only client at the time. The woman doing my toes suggested a darker color (I had a very pale pink) and even swatched them for me to show me how much more better my toes would look with the darker color. I thought that was really nice of her to do. My nails and toes look freaking amazing thanks to these two. A Mani and Pedi cost me $35, but it looks like they have variable pricing. My only complaint, which is soooo minor is that I wish they had a better polish selection. There were a boatload of pinks and reds but not too many pastels or "different" colors.

RANT

E. S., TX

They charge too much for their services in my mind. When you look at the prices, they don't look that bad, but when you actually get there, they are trying to get you out of there as fast as possible. It's a rush job that turns out alright but not very good quality for the price. They also do Mani and Pedi at the same time which makes you have to contort the whole time into uncomfortable positions and not get to relax or even take a sip of their "free drinks" that they are so proud of. I even just left with my hands sticky... how do your hands get sticky during a Mani? I don't even know. Overall, I'm very disappointed. If you are looking for a place to quickly get something done just to have something done, this might be the place for you. If you are looking for a relaxing, quality job, definitely go somewhere else.

RAVE

S.V.

The ladies will accept appointments and walk-ins, the salon is clean, they play easy-listening soft/pop music, and it's on a corner with floor-to-ceiling windows on the East & North sides. All make the experience mellow & pleasant, since the ladies are profes-sional yet not chatty or over-the-top smiley with the patrons. Which is fine; I flip thru their magazines, or bring a friend for a Pedi, or play on my smart-phone while enjoying the view outside: trees, lots of people watching.

RANT

C.R. New Hampshire

Very disappointed in the manicure I received. Within 24 hours the polish was peeling. I got the manicure so that my nails would look great for my vacation and the result was just the opposite.

RANT

D.M.

It's necessary for people to remember nail salons are providing a service. I've been to many different Asian owned salons and there is always a language barrier. How can you receive proper service if u can't be understood? If I'm paying for a service it should be done to my specifications. Many times I've either left or given up and let the manicurist do what they want because they couldn't understand my request.

RANT

K.N.

Some people complain and complain about the nail industry being saturated or dominated by Asians but I think they are brilliant people. They came over and found an occupation that pays bills and taxes, better than flipping burgers, they have their children here, who are true Americans. Ultimately America is all races, I mean well we took it from the Native Americans, she looked white as day so she really has no room to claim America America. And I can guarantee you any Asian owned nail salon can run circles around her on their funny looking brooms.

RANT

M.E., TX

This place was a "NIGHTMARE "this place had gel product that was defective which turn my manicure into a disaster. When I returned to get some help, Kay, the so called mgr. /owner was very rude and was not helpful. After stressing myself to get some help, Kay finally said "we take care now" ok, should of been done from the get go. This place is all about greed, selfishness, and absolutely no customer service experience and quality (F) very poor. I was practically going every 2 weeks, spending right at 100.00 per visit. Please do not spend your money, go elsewhere!

INTERNATIONAL

MCNY
Madrid,
Spain Nicole
P.

This place is absolutely amazing! The service is incredible and all the ladies are so attentive. The girls work well and quickly. The salon itself is beautifully decorated, bringing a very sophisticated New York vibe to the center of Madrid. They have a wide variety of services available, and for those looking to do their nails, you'll have hundreds of colors and brands to choose from. The only complaint I have is that the prices are a bit high in comparison to other salons in Madrid. Regardless, I think it's a great place and I'll definitely be back again.

RANT

A.O., TX

Unsatisfied!!! Today I took my Daughter for her 14th birthday and her 2 friends to get a set of acrylic nails. The techs that did the nails on the girls were upset & one of them was yanking at my Daughters friends fingers & rolling her eyes b/c she wouldn't relax her fingers. I had no idea of what was going on as I was in the front waiting for them. I paid, gave each of the techs a tip without knowing how they treated these girls. I wasn't told until we were ordering at a restaurant, that they told me their experience. I was so livid & took everything out of me not to get up & go back and let them hear me out. The girls said everyone around them were being offered a drink and they weren't even offered water. They hated their experience. So, if you take young ones, make sure they're offered/treated as a paying customer, not as a nuisance.

RAVE

J. S.

If you pass by this unassuming nail salon, stop and go in. It's everything you want -- cheap Mani/Pedi's, long massages, a sassy staff, and happy customers popping champagne and swapping stories about the night before. Bliss.

RANT

P. O., Oregon

I was JUST there, and I had a terrible experience. First my appointment was at 1 o clock and I didn't sit down in a chair until 1:20. I got acrylic French tips and there turned out to be bubbles all over it and the nail tech was completely oblivious to them. She told me there was nothing she could do about it, which is not true because I have gotten my nails done elsewhere, and it was much better at other places. I ended up having her take them off because I wasn't going to pay for something I wasn't happy with. Second I got a pedicure French tip, and it came out really bumpy looking, the tips were uneven and they forgot to give me sandals so I walked around bare footed to the drying station. I didn't end up leaving until almost 4 o clock. I was really upset that they had done so poorly because I have many friends that have been there multiple times without a problem at all.

RAVE

Lauren C.

I just moved to Glenview and was in need for a Mani/Pedi. I searched Yelp and thought I'd give Heavenly Nails a try after reading other reviews. I was not disappointed. I walked in (no appointment) on Sunday morning and was greeted by a woman whom I believe is the owner. Although their polish selection isn't the best, I was able to find a good variety of colors to choose from. A man technician, Long, greeted me at the pedicure station and offered me something to drink - which never happens at nail places. I immediately turned on the massage chair which was quite relaxing. While I was relaxing in the chair I noticed that the people around me getting their nails done seemed to be regulars. Also, the phone kept ringing of clients calling to make appointments (and group party reservations). All of this I took as a good sign -- Heavenly must have a good, repeat client base. The place is clean from what I can tell, and Long opened a new package of nail tools prior to beginning my services - which I was quite happy about. I paid $40 for a Mani/Pedi which I believe to be quite reasonable. I think they have a special if you go on Mon-Tue-Wed for $35. I also heard some women requesting to get their eyebrows & lip waxed, so they must be good for that too. Maybe next time I'll try an eyebrow wax. Long did a great job on my pedicure & manicure - both were very relaxing and he was very friendly. I'll definitely be going back to Heavenly.

RANT

R.H.

OMG they charged me $85.00 for regular acrylic nail and Pedi with airbrush flags that were terrible and looked at me crazy for the $5.00 tip as if they deserved more, they deserved ZERO!!! I would never return to their facility!!!

RANT

Mary C., MO

This used to be my go to nail salon. My last visit changed my mind about coming back. Customer service does not exist at this place. I requested one of my favorite technicians, Bryan, to give me a manicure and the receptionist told me to go get him from the back of the salon and tell him what I wanted done. This didn't come across as very professional. Also one of the technicians, an older lady, began clipping her own toe nails in the chair right next to me. Needless to say, that last visit was my last visit.

RANT

G.U.

Great job on eyebrows but my nails fell off four days later...

RANT

L. W., MO

DONT GO HERE I got a bacterial infection... my feet have been itching and burning w/red spots on them for two weeks.......I just don't want this to be ugly. : (

RAVE

D. V., IL

I LOVE this place. Although I just come in for the pedicures they do have an amazing Mon-Wed Mani/Pedi deal. The best in the area by far. They are always nice and talkative and the place is very clean and comfortable.

RAVE

P. L.

Love this place! Good thing I remember faces...because next time (later on today) I go there, I want the same lady helping me. BEST MANICURE EVER!! I tipped her just for the massage...and her eyebrow waxing skills are killer!! Go to this place...they take their time with you...they talk to you...and they are reasonably priced!! I guess I only gave them 4stars because I have little to compare them to...(except 'mini nail' down the street...which is awful)...I'm sure there are bigger and better places...but I like this one for now!!

RANT

L.G., IL

OMG looking at the pics I was like wow they do nice work, omg I get there to get Mani and Pedi, I could not believe it. A Pedi was putting my feet in a 20 dollar Conair foot massager didn't cut my nails or cuticles, came out with a bucket of dirty utensils and then leave that spot to go to a station to left my foot up on her knee to paint my nails 25 dollars NEVER again, stations are dirty. Rip off trust me anywhere else is better, so disappointed.

RAVE

S.B.

New favorite nail salon on the north side. A group of coworkers and I came here for a little girls' afternoon out and were quite pleased. The ambiance/decor is adorable, the owner is friendly (and funny), and the nail services were fantastic. We had a great time and we will be back!

RAVE

Kelly K.

Saw the wonderful reviews & decided to give this place a try. Called yesterday evening to make an appointment for today without any trouble & the girl on the phone was super sweet. I have been to nail salons on all different ends of the spectrum & let me say, this may be my favorite to date! Why did I like it?? *The staff is super friendly & very welcoming. They have a large assortment of both regular & no-chip colors. Even the neon & glitter colors*Very clean

& organized*my nail tech did an EXCELLENT job on my nails! :)
She was very thorough on both my hands & feet but was quick. I
got a polish change on my toes & a no-chip Mani and was in and
out in less than an hour*While your nails are drying the techs
give you a mini shoulder massage! *Simple decor & relaxing
music is wonderful*I usually like to zone out and relax during my
nail pampering time, so I don't usually talk too much. The tech
that I had was so sweet and didn't try to talk my ear off. During
my time there I saw several kids getting mini manicures &
pedicures. They got designs and it was adorable. I'm not a mom,
but I'm sure a lot of mom's would appreciate knowing that. lol.
Any Issues?? The one thing that might be an issue to some, is
that the front area where the waiting area, drying table & all of
the nail polishes are is pretty tiny & could get very tight on a
super busy day. I will defi-nitely be back & will highly recommend
this nail salon to anyone looking for a clean salon, a relaxing
atmosphere & an overall great experience!

RANT

Kate F.

Clean, pretty salon. Kind, attentive technicians. Nails and toes
looked okay when I left, though they switched the polish I picked
and the colors did not match as I had hoped. No chip manicures
typically last at least a week before starting to look a little rough
at the edges, but this Mani was chipping within three days. My
big-gest frustration was paying for a Pedi and leaving with still
rough heels!

RAVE

J. J.

I discovered Zaza when I was looking for a place to get my eyebrow threaded. They did a great job and the salon itself is very nice and luxurious feeling. I also love how they allow you to book appointments online. It makes it so much easier to plan out your day!

INTERNATIONAL

Culture of Color

Paris,

France Alice

D.

This salon is a GEM of a find in Paris. Very NYC style setup, clean, modern and the nail technicians are very well trained and very friendly. My French is minimal, and I was so happy that one of the girls was completely fluent in English. **Both Marion and Melanie are topnotch technicians** Friendly, polite and very patient with the clients. I would advise to book an appt. in advance. I walked in the first time and then made follow up appts. for the next 3 weeks. Enjoy and Merci Beaucoup merci à Marion et Melanie! I will def. be coming back on my next visit and highly recommend this location to anyone traveling or living in Paris who desires a première class Mani/Pedi at a reasonable price. J'adore Culture of Color à Paris!

RAVE

Ali F.

I'm obsessed with this place. I and my mom just happened to try this salon because our usual place was booked. I won't speak for my mom but I am loving the job they did! Like dying. I got a regular pedicure and everything was really clean and the technician took her time to really clean up my feet. For my hands, I actually got gel artificial nails (this isn't usual for me but recent stress has lead me to pick at and destroy my nails). OK, so Kim did the service and she is like my new favorite person. First of all, since the artificial nail process is more time consuming than a regular manicure, Kim actually took the initiative to get ahead and started on my nails while I was in the pedicure chair. (I digress, I totally felt like a celebrity getting my toes and hands done at the same time lol). As far as the job she did, I was impressed with how meticulous Kim was. She kept pausing to make sure I was liking what she did, like if the nails were the right length and the file shape right. When I couldn't decide which color to do on my nails Kim was very patient with me and painted each option on my nails so I could see how the color looked painted. Most of all, I am very happy with the final result, the nails are false, but look totally natural! Which is the look I was going for. And I love love love the color I settled on (OPI's Are You Ear for Van Gog-h). This place absolutely earned the five-star rating. I will definitely be back for sure!

RANT

Glenda P.

I have been going to _____ for over a year and I have had good experience till just recently. The Manager used to be Kelly who was very professional and respected the customers and their time. Recently they have changed management where this new management lacks the professional that I saw in this nail salon. I always enjoyed going there alone and with my friends and family, it was a relaxing and enjoyable place. Recently my experience has change where it is loud and there is always loud conversation among the workers in foreign language. But what made me write this review is my experience a few weekends ago where I made appointment for 4 people 4 days in advance. I was hoping for all of us to enjoy a little gathering at the Nail Spa. I arrived on time for my appointment and they struggled to get 3 of us. But they could not take me and after waiting 25 minutes after my appointment they asked me to wait another 15 min. I had to leave because I couldn't afford the additional time and there was no explanation on why they couldn't honor my appointment or even an apology. The Owner need to monitor this closely and bring back the profes-sional that the Salon had which made me change and start going to Heavenly Nail for the past year.

RAVE

Joann B.

About as good as it gets! I have never been in a nail salon that has been so welcoming and relaxing. You felt special the second you walked in - from being offered water to the massages to the own-ers getting to know you. The prices are very reasonable - I got a deluxe pedicure and a no-chip manicure for under $70. The pedi-cure itself was the best, most relaxing that I have ever had. The massaging was just insane. They must have gone for almost 20 minutes with the various scrubs and creams. They even used an actual orange for the mixture. My nail tech also made an awe-some suggestion for a no-chip color as well. The only reason I gave this place 4 stars was due to the up-selling culture. They kept on asking about eyebrows (yes, I know mine are hairy) and higher level pedicures. I get it, but this can definitely turn some people off.

RANT

Nikki E.

I'm unbelievably disappointed in this place. I drove here from the city with the hopes of finding my new "Go to" nail salon. Parking was a nightmare. To say this place is tiny and cramped is truly an understatement. The drying station and nail polish selection (which was severely limited) were one foot from one another. Some broad and her two kids hogged the entire spot to the point where I gave up and picked anything. And that was just the beginning. It was almost 90 degrees yesterday, and everyone but I and the young girl next to me were offered bottled water. Wtf? There was no price list, no list of services offered, the massage chair was on its last leg, and the tech cut me during my Pedi, and blamed it on my nails being long. I read the reviews and will chalk this up to new management. This place was so chaotic. I had to listen to the guy all the way across the room tell someone else across the room that his 13 year old son bites his toe nails. Eew. Yes folks, this is how I spent my Sunday. But really, the pedicure was rushed and had me stressed during the entire process. The girl working on me was really rough, unfortunately she didn't feel like I was worthy of a quality Pedi because when I got home I noticed that she didn't even scrub the entire bottom of my foot. Waste of time, money and gas. We are never ever getting back together.

RAVE

Susan S.

I have been to this nail salon a couple of times now and thought I should write a review for them. My daughter recommended this place and she is a licensed cosmetician and knows what to look for. I LOVE THIS PLACE. It is so clean and the instruments are brought to your station sterilized and sealed in the packet. The staff are very nice and attentive. They have 6 nail stations and 8 foot massage chairs for pedicures. My 2 week no chips last THREE weeks. I'm just like you, I wash dishes, pull weeds and garden, but I do wear gloves. I just trim and file and I'm good to stretch out another week. I was a little concerned about going to the no-chip because I know how busy I can be and was worried about the ability to maintain them. I've tried other salons and barely get 10 days' worth of nice nails. So between the quality of the technique and their product, plus their salon hours, I am there pretty regularly.

RAVE

J. S.

Just left Heavenly Nails & Spa and I loved it!!!!! They put a big smile on my wife's face. The service is amazing. We both got pedicures and she got her nails done. I must say hands down best experi-ence ever. Quinie was great. Thank you!!!!! We will definitely be back!! Great job guys.

RAVE

Cindy L.

I just went here yesterday for the first time and had a great experi-ence! I don't live in Chicago anymore so I don't really have a go-to nail salon when I'm in town (I only get my nails done every few months anyway) but _____Nails might be my new go-to! It was super easy to get in early on a Sunday - I called in first just to make sure they knew I was coming in. I got a gel manicure for $35 which is standard price around here. But I would say this was above and beyond the standard service for a gel Mani. The best part of the whole experience was how great they were at help-ing me find the right color. They have an amazing selection of gel colors, however, I am pretty particular about the color and I have been on an endless search for the perfect neutral whitish-pink that's not too pink. They knew exactly what I was looking for when
I described it and proceeded to layer colors until it was perfect! They took their time and were super nice, warm and welcoming when I walked in. They didn't try to sell me anything else at all and were genuinely interested in making sure I was happy when I walked out the door. Definitely returning here and definitely refer-ring this place to everyone I know!

RAVE

Nicole S.

Fabulous. Ultra clean. Fantastic work. Great staff. It's not your typical nail salon. Very calm, beautifully decorated, and a no-rush atmosphere. Best around!

INTERNATIONAL

Gentlemen's Tonic, Mayfair, London

As yet, men's manicures aren't offered in abundance but a number of London salons do provide them. Catering only to men, Gentlemen's Tonic is reassuringly – but unaggressive – masculine. Manicure clients sit cocooned in plush, leather, barbershop-style chairs, or lay in a darkened treatment room. The treatment itself sees fingernails filed, shaped, buffed and moisturized, and concludes with a relaxing hand massage. The effects are subtle – so much so, in fact, that men skeptical about the need for this type of treatment may remain unconvinced – but others will appreciate the discreet, looks-like-normal-but-better end results.

RAVE

Christie C.

Best nail salon in the north suburbs of Chicago that I've ever been to. I called ahead asking if I could come in the morning for a Mani & Pedi, they asked what time, I said within the next 15 minutes, and they were totally excited and said "see you soon." When I got there I was greeted by Tory, who was friendly from the beginning. She already knew when I walked in that I was the girl who called ahead. They already had a pedicure seat ready for me after I chose my colors, where Kevin did an awesome job with my pedicure and a great foot/leg massage. They also offered me something to drink, which was really nice. Tory worked on my no chip Mani while Kevin was finishing my toes, which was great because then I didn't have to wait too long. Tory's husband also added cute little flowers to my big toes & palm trees to my ring fingers, which wasn't an extra charge. I love how they make you feel welcomed right when you walk in and start conversation like they've known you for a while even though it was my first time going there. Tory even gave me an amazing back massage when I was waiting for my toes to dry. The reasonable price, cleanliness, atmosphere, and friendly staff are all great incentives for me to come back!

RAVE

Nancy G.

This place is absolutely AMAZING!!! From the second that we walked in the staff treated us like VIP. I started with the milk and honey Pedi. Talk about relaxation. Soft music, green tea, the best massage chairs and the most amazing foot rub from Kim was what I got. Then came time for my nails. Steven did an excellent job. He put a brand new set of gel nails on and shaped them perfectly. The design that he did was awesome. He ended with a great hand massage followed by a back massage that almost put me to sleep. Throughout the entire time we were there every staff member asked us how we were doing and if we were enjoying ourselves. The atmosphere itself was perfect, but to be in a place where you felt like a valued customer from beginning to end was exactly what I've been trying to find in a nail salon. I won't have to look any further because this is where I will be coming from now on. I highly recommend trying out Heavenly Nail & Spa.

RAVE

Paula L., IL

I was looking for a salon that had later hours because I was coming from the city, and I chose Heavenly Nails because it was the best location for me based on my Google search. I got there yesterday at 7:00 p.m., and the staff was as nice as could be. I got a beauti-ful pedicure and a no-chip manicure, and have been looking at my nails and smiling all day. They really have it all - friendly, profes-sional, TONS of colors to choose from, and they did a great job.

INTERNATIONAL

ARK Skincare's Anti-Aging Manicure, Putney, England

I was almost late for my appointment at ARK and arrived slightly stressed, having hotfooted it down Putney High Street. However, as soon as I stepped over the threshold and took in the heavenly smell of burning incense, I immediately recovered. The manicure uses ARK's own completely natural products, including an Exfoliating Body Scrub with loofah particles to remove any dead skin, followed by an Anti-Ageing Hand & Nail Cream rich in es-sential fatty acids, which was mixed with their Antioxidant Serum to reduce age spots. A soothing hand and arm massage was the cherry on the cake, and I was left with hands that looked like they belonged in a Fairy Liquid commercial.

RAVE

Kim L.

I randomly wondered into this place a few months ago to get a pedicure with a friend of mine and I have never had such a great pedicure. First off, they really know what they're doing because I have my big toe nails that grow downward and they tend to hurt. Everyone who works here who has done my pedicure has had no trouble at all dealing with this and no one has hurt me in the process. The massage given for the pedicure is like none I've ever experienced. They massage your legs and feet for I'd say a good 7 minutes each. It's heaven. They also put lotion on the scrubby thing when they scrub your feet and I think that's genius. I started coming here more and more often and also started getting mani-cures. They are fantastic and very precise. Never painful, always enjoyable. They also give you a shoulder massage during the manicure. All the people who work here are so nice and talented. It's always a pleasant visit when I go there. OH they also always offer you something to drink which I think is really nice. I recently moved about 30 minutes from here and it's definitely worth the drive, I'm going to continue to come here.

RANT

D.H., San Francisco

I had a good experience here once... I hate to say, I was very displeased with my eyebrows... they are different from each other in addition to she took hair off the top when I asked to keep them IF possible. Then I got a Mani Pedi where they had to redo one of my nails because she left some of the polish from my previous nails.... THEN the counter lady called me to tell me she gave me too much change and had to charge me and extra $34, I agreed since it was the right thing and said I would call after work. I got called three more times while in meeting and at a company party. My whole experience was doomed from the eyebrows since I was upset already... My first time nails were good and maybe it was a coincidence but was handled very unprofessional which proceeds me to never try this place again.

RAVE

V. Pham

I work in SOMA, and ____ nail spa on 2nd street is my favorite nail place. I think it's the one place where you can come in and truly relax. The place itself is very nice, clean, and inviting. The nail specialists know what they're doing, and they're very sweet. I speak to them in Vietnamese all the time when I am there; they are all wonderful. It is more expensive than other nail spas in the area BUT it's worth it. My nail polish lasts forever. I think it's the only nail spa I would truly recommend in the city, hands down.

RAVE

S. H.

____ is by far the best nail spa here in the Bay Area. They are definitely my go to place for nails, waxing, massages, and lashes!
No other places that I know of provide a clean and peaceful environment like they do. With their stainless steel bowls and new sanitized tools, why would anyone go anywhere else! They let you keep your file, buffer, and pumice pad too! Thank you for also providing amazing customer service.

RANT

M. Richards

It's weird here. I don't mind paying the extra bucks than what I'm used too. But I don't think they have ever had a blk customer before. Maybe I'm wrong. But the surprise they had on their faces. Lol. Anyways it was a last resort for me and they faked their dis-comfort the best they could. Give them an E for Effort.

RAVE

S.F.

Ignore the tacky 80's decor and the weird mismatching Pier1-esque cushions -- this place is the real deal. They're seriously dedicated to making your Mani/Pedi perfect and will go the distance to keep you happy. The free snacks help, too!

INTERNATIONAL

The Nail Loft at Urban Retreat, Harrods, Knightsbridge, England

Having recently undergone a revamp, Urban Retreat's Nail Loft is intended to resemble a Hermès bag – needless to say its manicures are super luxurious. First my nails were put under the spotlight with a preliminary nail consultation, which involved the therapist, Angel, assessing my weak, ragged nails with a raised (and perfectly plucked) eyebrow. She then instructed me not to buff my nails (as this will make them weaker), and prescribed a protein treatment and cuticle oil to apply each night. Angel was great company, and the Immaculate Manicure that followed, involving a delightful hand massage and hot mitts, was a treat from start to finish.

RAVE

Jennifer H., San Francisco

I love heading over to Pinkies in Potrero Hill for my idea of a relaxing happy hour--getting a manicure and pedicure while shopping for on-trend fashion jewelry. The setting of the salon is great because it is more than just a nail salon. It truly is a spa boutique with large displays of necklaces, bracelets, rings, and earrings carefully cu-rated and decorated amongst the salon. As far as nail services, I love how they have by far the largest collection of gel nail polish colors in all of San Francisco--they must have over 50 different shades. The staff is amazingly sweet and attentive and really make you feel like you are a guest in their nail-boutique-of-happiness.

RANT

R.F.

This is not all it's cracked up to be. You can get a better job done at your normal corner nail shop and pay less with more of a selec-tion. They are racist and treat you good only if you are the same color as the owner who isn't as nice as he seems. I called and he answered the phone "what is it that you want" I didn't even waste my time making another appt. that was it for me. The only reason I wanted another appt. was for a waxing because I found a better place to get my nails and feet done for way less. DONT GO TO_____!!!!

RANT

P.R.

I am a _____ regular and I go there at least once a week. They have a 5-star excellence service and a lot of accessories. There is one thing that I am very disappointed is that there are some mysterious charges. I've been here since the last owner and they never charge a penny in tax, but now they do. I complained about it, and they stopped charging tax. Now, they charge about $1.50 for San Francisco Health Care or San Francisco Health Plan, and they say that the charges are to cover health-care for their em-ployees. That's fine!!! But you know what? When I ask their em-ployees if they have health-care coverage, which is provided. The answers are, "We have never had health-care" & "I am covered by the company where my husband is working" & "I am paying for my own health-care". So, what are the charges for? A MYSTERY.

_____ are excellence but beware of the mysterious charges. If you see a mysterious charges, ASK!!! If they say the benefit go to their employees, ASK their employees, but don't let the manager or the owner know because the employees may get in trouble or even fired for answering the truth. I am keeping their receipts for fur-ther reference if I need to file any legal action against them. I will speak to the owner about the mysterious charges, and I will know what those mysterious charges are.

RANT

Ginny

Yeah... I won't be coming back here. I've gone to my share of nail salons, fancy ones, dingy ones, and really I care about 1 thing, you get what you pay for. I don't expect amazing service if I'm paying $20 for a Mani Pedi, but for $24 Pedi, and $34 Mani Pedi for my friend - I expected a LOT more than I got from KT. A couple tips: Don't bother making an appointment. While I was there, 2 people walked in with appointments at 3, and both just left out of frustration since there was 1 person working and 4 people who were there at 3. I later watched them answer the phones and take down more appointments, but not write anything down. Yeah... appointments aren't going to count for much here. File only! They cut your nails wayyyy too short! On one toe, she cut my nail so short, I'm still wincing when I walk. When I told her it hurt, she glared and said "That hurts?" Always ask upfront what the cost is. They don't have their prices listed anywhere, and from the reviews I'm seeing, they ask you to pay what they're feeling like that day.

RAVE

J.T.

Excellent service, very relaxing, and most importantly, all the champagne and mimosas you can drink. I go here way more often that I need to just for the experience.

RAVE

J. Bell, LA

I went last weekend, and I made an appointment before walking in. They did my deluxe pedicure! I even brought my male friend with me. He totally enjoyed the experience!!! Since we made an appointment, there was no waiting!!! The prices were slightly above average, but you get what you pay for!

INTERNATIONAL

A NAILS

Berlin,

Germany D.D.

Reliable & friendly nail salon. From a simple manicure / pedicure to shellac or gel nails, they have it all covered. I would advise call-ing & making an appointment, but walk-ins are usually possible without too much waiting time. The only issue I have is the lack of English knowledge. I have had to translate for non-German speak-ers on several occasions. Still, I come here all the time and not once have I been disappointed!

RANT

Gigi T.

Went to use a gift certificate only to find upon paying that they required the $50 to be used all at once, yet this wasn't written on the gift certificate. They also said it would be a 10 minute wait and kept me waiting for 35 minutes to get started. The entire time I was getting my nails done, the girl sat and chatted with another random girl who came in but was not getting any services done. The conversation was inappropriate, made me uncomfortable, and was completely unprofessional. Not to mention that I don't want to sit there for 45 minutes and listen to you converse about your boyfriends. My nails looked good at the end, but it was definitely not worth the terrible service and unprofessional atmosphere. Will never go back.

RANT

Lisa S., LA

Overpriced for shoddy work. Went there for a pedicure which took an unusually long time to dry, either because the polish was too thinned out or because they put my feet under a UV light with no fan. As soon as I put my shoes on after about 40 minutes of wait-ing, the polish got smudged. I wouldn't have minded any of this, except it cost me money and I could have just messed up my own toenails for free.

RANT

Brenda L.

This salon is a block away from my house so I was really excited to try it out. Everything was going well until they messed up a part of my pedicure. The tech sloppily painted over it with another color. You could see smears and drops of the other color. I asked her could she start over and redo the nail, she said no and told me to keep watching television! I could have cried. As I looked down at my nails I knew I couldn't allow myself to pay $33 for this and keep my messed up toenails. I asked another tech to please redo that particular nail and she did. They were so rude, just smiling, laugh-ing and talking amongst themselves when I asked a question. I was polite, respectful and felt completely ignored. I hate poor customer service and will not return or recommend this place to another person. And yes I did leave a tip despite the poor service.

RANT

Pam C.

Poor service .The ugly girl name Lisa was horrible, she talked too much, act like Asian bitch, and cannot stand her. I never come back. I cannot stand when you come to beauty salon but being served by an ugly looking girl uhhhhhhhhh

RAVE

Carol W., CO

I love an affordable salon that does great quality nails. Hard to find! I usually get the gel nails and they last a long time. They will fix them if they mess up before 7 days. Good color selection too. I get the basic pedicure and it includes a great hot stone massage. One of the guys has done my nails both times I've been and they do an excellent job and are fun to converse with. I also like that there is good ventilation in the salon. Other salons in the area should really consider some fans or opening the door.

RAVE

Karen G.

Very sanitary, they will open up the disinfected tools from their packages right in front of you before starting. I guess there was a little bit of a mix up initially, I originally had a lady who was going to work with me but one of the male technicians doesn't do male pedicures so they had to switch off with my husband. The male who did my pedicure was pretty awesome though. I would highly recommend their deluxe pedicure!! It was one of the best that I've had in a while. I'm very ticklish which can sometimes be a problem since I have to hold back from kicking the person when they try to scrub my feet, but this guy knew what he was doing and I barely squirmed in my seat. The only down side was that I was the last person in my group to start the pedicure but the first to finish. My feet are by no means jacked up but it would've been nice to get a longer massage. There was a different lady who pained my nails. She did a pretty decent job. She also did my manicure. Nothing spectacular, and there wasn't any arm massage involved but she still got the job done and tried to accommodate my needs.

RAVE

Andrea G.

I just went to JC Nails and I am very happy with the finished product. The girl that worked on my nails actually listened to me. These nails are pretty important to me, as I am getting married in a week. I have teeny tiny nail beds (the pink part of my natural nail is abnormally short) but I wanted a beautiful French manicure that didn't leave half of my (already pretty short) nail white. She did a natural nail color, and then whitened the tips. I was extremely happy since my little bitty nail beds were covered, and I still got the French manicure that I wanted. Other manicurists that I have seen never listen and they don't try to help me find a solution to my problem nails. If she could make me happy, I am pretty sure she could make anyone happy. I wish I had gotten her name. Ugh!

RAVE

M.T.

Lovely job on my pedicure! $22 includes a short hot stone massage and is a fantastic value. Very friendly staff and clean pedicure bowls. I think this would be a 5 star service if not for a run-down strip mall location in the not-so-nice part of Colorado Springs.

INTERNATIONAL

Singapor
e G.O.

Terrible terrible terrible and absolutely appalling. I'm sick on a Friday and probably won't be able to enjoy my weekend thanks to 2 very helpful staff at the Nail Spa. Having been able to rush down only after work, I approached the 2 staff and asked if they would be able to accommodate a full pedicure. They told me that since it was 8:15 pm and that they were closing at 9 pm and that a full pedicure would take an hour, it was out of the question that a full pedicure would be possible. So I settled for an express manicure and pedicure that ended at 9:40 p.m. Throughout my entire visit there, one of the staff was apparently very ill and kept coughing and sneezing and sniffling. At first, I thought it was ok that she wore a mask but honestly, she pulled it down her face exposing her nose and the top of her mouth, before she eventually took it off and just kept sneezing and coughing in close proximity to me and my face as she worked on my feet. I was appalled that you would allow your staff to work in close proximity to customers in such an intimate service line when they're evidently sick out of their heads and apparently don't mind spreading on the germs too. Express manicure and pedicure.

140 bucks. Great price! For contracting a free virus too. She didn't even bother to soak my feet. And honestly, I've been to GREAT places where they have wonderful service even at the express level. Needless to say, this was a very disappointing visit. I saw them opening the cupboards to take their things towards closing time and saw that they actually had tea for customers of which apparently my 140 express dollars were too cheap to warrant one. Your staff didn't even ask. Also, although I was sitting on a massage chair, I asked one girl, Nicole or something, if I could

turn it on, and she said no, the massage function on the chair can only be utilized if I do a full pedicure. So I said, you guys refused to let me do a full pedicure, she said they had no time. No time eh? Express manicure/ pedicure dragging to 9:40 p.m. from 8:15 p.m. because other than sick girl doing my toes I was worrying about spreading her germs, Nicole did a really bad job of doing my nails.

RAVE

April W.

I went here for the first time at a friends' behest and it was great! Affordable Pedi, friendly staff and service was great! Plus they do a 7 day polish guarantee and had a military discount. I think I just found my salon!

RAVE

Brenna A.

Best nail spot in Colorado Springs, especially for the price! I've been here 3 times in the last few months for the $35 deluxe pedicure and have always been pleased. Good selection of OPI polishes. The employees are friendly and conscientious, and the owner is very welcoming. Your pedicure starts off with a warm foot soak while you sip on your choice of non-alcoholic beverage. The deluxe pedicure is very pampering, with the usual cleaning/cal-lous removal to begin, then paraffin wax, hot towels, a foot and leg massage with lotion, and hot stones application. This is all topped off with a beautiful polish job. You can add your choice of designs for $7 more--I just did white polka dots on my dark purple polish for Spring Break. Suggested by my pedicurist and very cute! As others have mentioned, don't let the location on Academy deter you--it is clean and sanitary inside. JC Nails also offers a punch card for repeat customers, as well as military & student discounts. I will be back for another pedicure in a month or two to usher in summer. I have never had a manicure here but I would like to try the gel nails for vacation!

RAVE

Victoria C.

My family is in town visiting, so we decided to have a "girl's day". Soo happy I came across this place on Yelp!!!! There were 4 of us so I made an appt., they got us in right on time and did an amazing job!!!! We got manicures and pedicures, and they felt and look awesome!! Another added bonus is how friendly, clean and professional they are!! Will def. be back!! :-)

RAVE

Kristy L.

Reviews led me to this place and, hands down, this was THE BEST NAIL SALON I have ever been to in my 30 years of existence on this Earth. I wish they were in Denver, as I'm not from the Springs and was visiting family and had some time to kill. Will DEFINITELY make this place a must-stop when I visit from now on. Walked-in and immediately greeted by two friendly staff members. Asked for Shellac removal and manicure. I was then led to a station and immediately offered a drink (never had that happen before, how nice). They were eager to start on my Broncos-themed colors :) The staff are extremely friendly, knowledgeable, upfront and hon-est, articulate, and make it a point to engage with you in friendly English banter (I'm sure they'd let you sit and relax in silence as well). None of that "say three words to you" then turn around and say something in another language, leaving you wondering and paranoid. My nails came out beautiful. He was fast and efficient, yet precise. If you're not satisfied or something is wrong with your nails, they will fix it free of charge within a week! On a side note, I am a stingy tipper, I'll admit. Gave a $10 tip for a $25 Shellac manicure. Jimmy was more than deserving. Thank you again and see you soon!!

RAVE
Hammer & Nails Hand & Foot Grooming Shop
Los Angeles, CA
H.C.

This place puts the MAN in Mani/Pedi!

...but for sake of confidentiality, I'll just say that I may or may not know a guy who I may or may not have brought here. But I do hope that places like this will break down social judgments about com-promising masculinity. Ain't nothing wrong with proper grooming for men! Okay, okay, I get it. Most nail salons are girly and some men may feel like it's a girly activity. Some men may not be into girly activities. That's when I saw this place on Shark Tank adver-tising their man-cave atmosphere and I thought "this is perfect!"
I may or may not have made an appointment for a guy that I may or may not know. But let's just say, hypothetically, that there was this guy that I brought here and I ordered him the Hand & Foot Maintenance Combo. He was a bit confused at first but as soon as he sat down in the cushy leather seats, put on the headphones, and had remote in hand for his personal flat screen TV, he looked right at home. There is a small wooden bench in a waiting area near the front entrance where I planned to settle for the next hour.

But as soon as they began service on this hypothetical guy that I may or may not know, the staff gave me a cushion to sit on and offered to get me a drink. I think it was super sweet of them to take care of me as much as they were taking care of hypothetical guy. In fact, after waiting about 5 minutes, they invited me to have a seat in one of the cushy chairs. I wasn't expecting that at all and I'm not even sure if they would normally do that but I think our timing was good as they didn't have any other customers coming in for the rest of the day.

As Natasha worked on hypothetical guy's pedicure, she asked if I would be interested in getting my nails done too. Luckily I was in major need of a manicure and they happened to have the staff available. So Deja came over and gave me one of the classiest manicures I've ever had. It was just a basic dark color polish but something about the finished result just seemed so slick and classy! Their nail polish selection may be limited (less than 10 options) but I did find something that I liked in my favorite brand, Zoya. I really enjoyed the cushy chair, personal flat screen TV and headphones so I could watch Donut Challenge on The Food Network while getting my nails done. In many ways, I would prefer this place over my regular girly nail salon. Natasha, Deja, and a few other staff members whose name I didn't get were all so super sweet, friendly, and helpful! As for hypothetical guy who I may or may not know, he was very happy with his Hand & Foot Maintenance Combo. We even had a conversation after we left, noticing how detailed and particular Natasha and Deja were. They do a much better job here than other girly nail salons that I've been to. The prices are a bit higher on the spectrum of nail salon prices but it is worth it in service and atmosphere. Would I come back here? Absolutely! ...and I'm pretty sure a guy that I may or may not know will want to return too :).

RAVE

NY, NY

Donna P.

Bed of Nails is the BEST! I absolutely love this place. They do amazing nail art. They have every nail color under the sun and no matter what nail pic I pull off my Pinterest board Candice (owner) will perfectly execute it. I'm not big on writing reviews but I have to give Bed of Nail BIG! Props because my nails are always hands down gorgeous when I walk out of there. Go uptown, it's worth it.

RAVE

Alameda, CA

C.S.

Superior nail spa:

*Amazing service: offering water, tea, just plain warm and professional *Fantastic products, they have every professional line you can think of and ones not on your radar*If you're into all the crazy blinged out nails a la Tokyo, it's here, people travel an hour for this stuff, they are complete pros*They hear their clients and respond appropriately*Technicians are knowledgeable about ALL things nail, every visit has been an education for me, special tools are used for individualized concerns and their callous removal system is beyond effective*Staff go to regular training and industry events, these are career professionals*Cutting edge: not just UV lights for gel, LED also*Can't believe it's on a deserted random street on the outskirts of Chinatown = easy parking Prices are definitely a little higher, but you get what you pay for. My pedicure was THE best I have EVER had, ANYWHERE, hands down. The shape, the color application, the massage, the non-tacky lotion, no detail is left astray, all culminate to the longest lasting polish. I am the CHEAPEST person about Mani/Pedi's. This is worth it.

RAVE

Oakland,

CA B. Y.

I'm one of those people who hops around when it comes to nail salons. I've had a lot of great Mani/Pedi's and I've met a lot of sweet nail ladies. The reason I hopped around was because I never do anything fancy - no nail art, no glitter, and no crazy colors. I keep my nails natural most of the time. They're short and if I get a manicure I will maybe do gelish/shellac polish in a light pink or a dark, dark purple. But this place is hands down, the BEST place to go and get a manicure. After going here I realize how amaz-ing my nails could actually look. My nails were filed in a beautiful shape and this shellac manicure lasted a MONTH. No lie. I felt like I could start a career as a hand model after walking out of this place. George Castanza status. I asked for a gift certificate here for Christmas because I all I want for 2016 is a monthly Mani at Cosmo Spa Lounge. Can't wait to go back!

RAVE

Oakland,

CA CAT

F.

So this review is SOOOOO long overdue! The reason I came here is because I had horrible nails due to wearing acryl-ics for over 15 years and this was the only place that offered the Bio Sculpture Gel nail system. Now if you're wonder-ing what Bio Sculpture Gel is then I give you a quick run thru.

This system is 100% natural and healthy for your nails. I know in-credibly hard to believe but it's true! That a gel system is good for your nails. Well for starters this gel is not acrylic based like shellac. Second my nails were paper thin and looked really unhealthy even with a shellac Mani but, after 2 years of religiously using only this my nails are strong and beautiful again! Don't believe me, then Google and YouTube this stuff.

Ok so now that I have gushed over my love for this product on to my review. Cosmo is honestly the most amazing nail place I have ever been too! Total spa atmosphere and totally relaxing. All the ladies are lovely and amazing talented. I'm not into nail art but these gals got some serious skills. Jenn is my go to gal I love her. Seeing her is like meeting with a girlfriend for lunch. She is amazing and talented and has been doing nails for over 20 years. Her manicures are always perfect. But honestly all the ladies are great. If you want a truly relaxing experience than get your tush down to Cosmo and enjoy your pamper time! ;)

RANT

Albany,

CA Paula

It may just be the one girl - Tina, but she sprayed my nails with something to help the nails stick. And forgot to dry them before putting the glue on, and the pain was so bad I was screaming! Like someone was stabbing my nails. Next time I went she didn't have much time as she was expecting an appointment, so she was rushing like mad, so I said I didn't want to continue if she was going to rush like that as I didn't want to pay for a bad job. I am looking elsewhere now.

INTERNATIONAL

Four Seasons Nail and Spa

Toronto,

Canada Kat F.

I stumbled upon this place while coming back from a doctor's appointment and I'm so glad I did. Tucked away just steps away from Royal York subway in Etobicoke, Four Seasons (not affiliated with the hotel chain) is an amazing nail bar. The Japanese and Korean ladies that run the place work tirelessly to treat several dozen women at a time, simultaneously doing your manicure AND pedicure - meaning you're out the door in 30-40 minutes instead of having to wait separately for one person to do each set of nails. The salon uses Essie and OPI polishes and there is a positively MONSTROUS selection available. We're easily talking 100+ co-lours. Any colour you can imagine. I highly recommend Cajun Shrimp, Big Apple Red, Lincoln Park After Dark (duh) and Russian Navy.

RANT

Starkville,

MS Amy R.

I went in yesterday for a full set of acrylic nails and while the staff there is nice enough, I left with 6 of my 10 nail beds bleeding...
no apology no anything. My fingers are so sore this morning it's terrible. I won't go back and if you value your safety where that's concerned you won't either. Those dremel type tools they use don't belong in a nail solon, they belong in a car body shop.

RAVE

E.N.

"Es" stands for elegant satisfaction and with their first nail salon location in Shibuya, Tokyo, they have been providing just that since 2003. Located in Beverly Hills, these nail art specialists pro-vide a variety of decoration services which are provided in large, comfortable areas that have a relaxed, Japanese style. Es Nails understands that nails are an extension of your style and part of fashion and they promise to make your "nail life more beautiful, prettier and sparklier."

RANT

Ridgeland,
MS Trista T.

My mother went in to get a pedicure and was asked to the back only to be asked her weight then told there was a weight limit and she was over that limit. Therefore they could not do her pedicure but had the audacity to tell her they could do a manicure for her with no problems. And the ONLY reason she went was because I used to frequent the salon. Most horrible experience for my moth-er!!!! The only recommendation I'd give would be for everyone to find another salon. FOREIGN owned but in the US mistreating us. SHAMEFUL!!

RANT

San

Diego M.

S.

1.5 stars: missed steps, bad French tip, no massage, musical chairs. Came here with three other girls. Saw great reviews on yelp and it was in the area we wanted. Also they had gel nails at a steal price $25! I'm guessing they named themselves "Trio Nails" because there are 3 ladies working. Expecting one of us to sit out, I was surprised when their played musical chairs and had a different worker on each step of the manicure process. I don't know about you, but I like it when one person works on my nails because it feels more personable and they start to develop a small relationship with your nails getting to know shape, thick-ness, etc. Obsessed with nail polish and manicures, I've been to my fair share of nail salons and was disappointed when they started my manicure without soaking it to soften the cuticles. The other girls said that they got that... maybe that step of mine was forgotten since they were playing musical chairs? One of the ladies proceeded to start cutting my nails and filing it and pushing back my DRY cuticles and cutting the hang nails. Great. After applying the gel polish, French tip, and then gel top coat, I already noticed that my right thumb didn't have a straight line and the white color was bleeding into the clear. The thumb is the most important fin-ger... The gel dries almost instantly in 3 minutes under the UV light which is good since I usually accidently smear it or mess it up. I didn't get that five minute massage that they usually do with warm lotion at other nail salons. Business wasn't even busy besides my girls and I so there shouldn't be any excuse. I expected to be there at least 2 hours but only spent 45 minutes on all 4 of us, which is good but I prefer quality over quantity. With tip included the total for French gel nails was $30. I think next time I'll pay the extra $10 and get a better one elsewhere.

RAVE

San

Francisco

Abbey

One of the most affordable Mani/Pedi's I've experienced. $27! That's practically free... Make an appointment if you don't want to wait for 20 or so minutes, there's only 2 ladies working. Complimentary snacks, water, and tea go a long way. And I get a kick out of the electric blue water with lemon slices used for pedicures! No massage chairs or lengthy massage as you get a regular service. However you can pay $10 or $20 for an extended service. Smart thinking. I will be back!

RAVE

Japantown, San

Francisco Gary K.

They made my girlfriend's toes look so yummy I wanted to eat her feet!! She is super happy and asked me to leave a 5 star review because these ladies earned it! We highly recommend this place and their prices are more than fair and they did it in no time!

INTERNATIONAL

Culture of Color

Paris, France

Bethany W.

I loved this nail bar! Being from Los Angeles, I am used to there being a nail salon on every corner and being able to walk in any time. Here you will definitely need to make an appointment a day or two in advance (unless you get lucky!) But it's worth the wait! I went in with a gel manicure already on my hands so first my mani-curist wrapped my hands in the cotton soak and foil to remove the polish. With my hands wrapped I was then moved to the pedicure chair for a very nice pedicure. Chair was comfy and had a good massager. After my pedicure was done, I moved back to the nail bar where my manicurist removed my gel polish and did a new gel manicure. I would have liked a little bit longer massage, but maybe that's just what I'm used to in the states. Overall my experience was excellent. Really cute little shop, good music, nice employees, beautiful selection of colors. It was nice to take a respite from sightseeing for a bit of pampering!! Cash or credit card!

RANT

Sandy W.

They market themselves as an 'urban pit stop' in the heart of Soho, and their flexible booking system makes them just that. You can pop in even if they're fully booked, and you usually won't have to wait more than ten minutes for a slot. Instead of being seated at a table, a cushion and towel were placed over my lap to create a' work surface' before the manicure began. (The Primark labels on the towels didn't exactly scream that this would be a luxury experience either.) Although my therapist was polite, the palpable pettiness among the rest of the staff reminded me of my second-ary school days. One of them told a shy new girl to clear up all the glasses 'as she was so talented at it.' I was happy with my nails but relieved to get out of there.

INTERNATIONAL

Mwnails, Shoreditch, UK

Around the 1970s, long before the era of the 'bucket flight', air travel was seen as the height of sophistication. That same vibe is echoed by MwNails whose interiors are made using actual parts of a Boeing 737 jet, while downstairs the pedicure area is furnished with first class Air France seats. The whole salon exudes a fun '70s vibe, with the nail technicians sporting vintage air hostess outfits, complete with pillbox hats. The treatments themselves are listed on a 'departures board' with names like Perfect Panama and Monte Carlo Minx. Carried away by the surroundings, I chose a fun bright orange OPI shade that really popped and I left the salon on a sugar high.

Chapter 9

CONCLUSION

The example set by the Vietnamese in the nail care industry is inspiring and praiseworthy. As fleeing refugees they did not come to America with a detailed business plan for the growth, develop-ment and expansion of what was in 1975 a sleepy trade bundled with beauty salon hair care services. Then, manicures and pedi-cures were provided by appointment only and could cost $50-60 with a limited selection of nail polish colors. The now iconic nail salon is a stand-alone nails business model Made in the USA.

The business was created on the foundation of compassion, hard work and foresight of Tippi Hedren, Becky and Charles Hambelton, Minh and Kien Nguyen and 20 pioneer manicurists including Thuan Le, and Yen Rist. Countless volunteers also made contribu-tions. Together, they created a path toward jobs and business own-ership, entrepreneurship and assimilation. Legions of immigrant manicurists followed and the Vietnamese came to dominate the nail care industry. At the same time, their efforts provided career role models for white, black, red and yellow women of other races and ethnic groups who later entered the manicuring field as entre-preneurs. The Vietnamese nail salon is more than a stereotype. It is an archetype!

Manicures cost $50.00-$60.00 in 1975 before the Vietnamese started salon businesses. Adjusted for inflation, a manicure could cost $400.00 today. Instead a manicure is possible for under

$25.00 because of the intervention in nail care history. As a result, the luxury of a manicure and pedicure is financially well within the reach of working class women. Thus countless manicuring and manufacturing jobs have been created. The economy was stimulated. Nail art as a fashion accessory and expression of personal style exists not only on high fashion runways but on the hands and feet of ordinary (but extraordinary) working class women.

The success of the nail salon business is a result of empowering women with skills and education. The success also demonstrates the value of welcoming newcomers to America, the home of im-migrants. As a result, the Vietnamese currently hold 51% of the manicuring trade in America's 8-billion-dollar nail care industry. There are a number of factors, theories and considerations to explain how the Vietnamese came to dominate the manicuring trade:

The Vietnamese have strong family values. From financial funding to operation, nail salons are family businesses with members working together to achieve a common goal. Female owners are prevalent, and they are supported by staff including husbands, children, relatives and extended family. It also helps that nail salon infra-structure provides flexibility for child care.

Vietnamese have tight knit communities and enclaves based on traditions, common background and experiences. Everyone knew someone who was in the business. There were plenty of success-ful role models, mentors and teachers to provide an emotional and financial cushion for budding female--and male--entrepreneurs seeking to enter the manicure field.

Religion may also have played a role. Many Vietnamese practice Buddhism, Confucianism or Taoism. These traditions encourage a collectivist rather than an individualist view of reality in which the group, the family, takes priority over fulfillment of individual needs and wants.

Technology played a role. The development of the acrylic nail in the 1980s provided a boost in the manicuring trade. It was some-thing new for women to try out and to indulge in.

The timing of Vietnamese entry into the nail care market is another possible factor. In 1975 women still wore only skirts or dresses to work in corporate office settings. Yet, they were entering the work force in greater numbers and they felt an increased interest in appearances. At the same time unemployment was very high and jobs were difficult to find. Job lay-offs were common. In addition, in some cases federally funded financial assistance was granted for three years only.

Many Americans and other immigrant groups regarded manicuring as a lowly profession. This attitude created a void which became an opportunity. Turning to nail care proved to be the strategy for economic survival; self-employment was the vehicle. Hence, the creation of the Vietnamese ethnic niche.

Vietnamese are hard-working people. Many nail salons are open seven days a week for more than eight hours per day. Perhaps, in part because the Vietnamese are hard-working, competition within the field is intense. It may be necessary for businesses to remain open longer to attract available customers. This may be especially true as competition fueled lower service prices. As competition increased it became necessary for manicurists and salons to move to fresh territories and markets within the United States and abroad. Many manicurists had family mem-bers in Vietnam, England, Australia and other countries; trans-national ties spawned global networks with salons around the world. Furthermore, competition may have had a bearing on the stimulation of technologies and products which allowed for faster and more efficient services.

Manicuring is a skill requiring inexpensive training, and nail salons have low start-up costs. Manicuring as an occupation was adopted and adapted as a means of survival. Lack of English fluency fueled discrimination and joblessness.

Creativity is a factor in the success of Vietnamese nail salons.

Vietnamese nail salons provide quality services at affordable prices.

Vietnamese manicurists are just plain good at what they do!

There has been an impact on education in addition to the impact on economy and culture. Few official polls or academic studies have been taken to document the number of Vietnamese-American doctors, lawyers and engineers whose education was funded by their mothers and fathers working in nail salons. The number would be greater perhaps than that inspired or resourced by any other business enterprise. It has been speculated that this emphasis on education results from Vietnamese family, culture, religion and ethics.

The Beat goes on

Family networks and transnational ties continue to inspire youth in Vietnam to come to America seeking the opportunities their elders found. The average age of a citizen in Vietnam is 25. The average age of an American citizen is 55. That's why immigrants should be welcomed! The Vietnamese nail salon business is a clear example of the economic impact immigrant entrepreneurs can have on a host society. Service sectors like nail care continue to outpace manufacturing sectors. Further, the intellectual knowledge base that comes with a youthful population can provide a refreshing contribution to America's aging national population. There is hope that fresh eyes may perceive, innovate and create new technolo-gies in wondrous entrepreneurial endeavors to solve contempo-rary problems and abuses.

Social scientists predict that in future decades, growth in the global labor force will be accounted for almost entirely by ethnic minorities. Even today, minority immigrant entrepreneurship exceeds that of the majority culture in most host countries. Of those minorities, women will comprise half of the globe-trotting immigrants. The Vietnamese nail salon business demonstrates that the empowerment of women with education and skill can have significant results for individuals, families, communities and countries.

Empowerment of women should be encouraged. According to *The World's Women 2010: Trends and Statistics* compiled by the United Nations organization, a full two-thirds of the world's women can neither read nor write. They have few marketable skills. Their minds, abilities and contributions remain untapped and dormant. Men have helped and must continue to help eliminate gender in-equality. A bird can no more fly with one wing than civilization can soar with gender inequality. According to Abdu'l-Baha, "As long as women are prevented from attaining their highest possibilities, so long will men be unable to achieve the greatness which might be theirs."

BIBLIOGRAPHY

Abdu'l-Baha. *Paris Talks (1912)*. Wilmette: U.S. Baha'i Publishing Trust, 1995.

Adams, Amy. "Survey Takes Health Snapshot of Nail Salon Workers." *Stanford Story Bank*, May 28, 2008.

Aggarwal, R. "Globalization of the World Economy: Implications for the Business School." *American Journal of Business* 23, no. 2 (2008): 209-20.

Bagwell, S. "Transnational Family Networks and Ethnic Minority Business Development." *International Journal of Entrepreneurial Behavior & Research* 14, no. 6 (2008).

Bagwell, S. "UK Vietnamese Businesses: Cultural Influences and Intra-cultural Differences." *Environment and Planning: Government and Policy* 24, no. 1 (2006): 51-69.

Barnes, E., L. Beck, and Et Al. *Milady Standard Nail Technology*. 7th ed. Accessed 2014. http://www.milady.cengage.com/cosmetology.asp.

Benzing, C., H. M. Chu, and G. Callahan. "A Regional Comparison of the Motivations and Problems of Vietnamese Entrepreneurs." *Journal of Developmental Entrepreneurs* 10, no. 1 (2005).

Bhagwati, J. *In Defense of Globalization*. New York: Oxford University Press, 2004.

Bordo, S. *The Male Body: A New Look at Men in Public and Private*. New York: Farrar, Straus and Giroux, 1999.

Brat, I. "Officials Target Nail Salons in Crackdown on Cleanliness." *Wall Street Journal* (New York), August 23, 2005, Eastern ed., D4 sec.

Brenner, G. A., L. J. Filion, and T. V. Menzies. "Problems Encountered by Ethnic Entrepreneurs: A Comparative Analysis Across Five Ethnic Groups." *New England Journal of Entrepreneurship* 9, no. 2 (Fall 2006): 25-35.

"Bridal Nail Art." Pinterest.com. November 9, 2014. http://www.pinterest.com/ nailartgallery/bridal-wedding-nail-art/.

Brindley, C. "Barriers to Women Achieving Their Entrepreneurial Potential: Women and Risk." *International Journal of Entrepreneurial Behavior & Research* 11, no. 2 (2005): 144-61.

Brocheux, P. *Ho Chi Minh: A Biography*. Cambridge University Press, 2007.

Cecilia, M. "Immigrant Kinship Networks: Vietnamese, Salvadorians and Mexicans in Comparative Perspective." *Journal of Comparative Family Studies* 28, no. 1 (1997): 1-24.

Chan, C. M., S. Makino, and T. Isobe. "Interdependent Behavior in Foreign Direct Investment: The Multi-level Effects of Prior Entry and Prior Exit on Foreign Market Entry." *Journal of International Business Studies* 37, no. 5 (2006): 642-44.

Chen, W. "Spinning Transnational Webs: Ethnic Entrepreneurship in the Internet Age." PhD diss., University of Toronto, 2008. Abstract in Dissertation Abstracts.

Chu, H. M., L. Zhu, and A. Chu. "Immigrant Business Owners: A Case Study of Vietnamese Entrepreneurs in America." *Journal of Business and Entrepreneurship* 22, no. 2 (October 2010): 60-74.

Collins, J., and A. Low. "Asian Female Immigrant Entrepreneurship in Small and Medium-sized Businesses in Australia." *Entrepreneurship & Regional Development* 22, no. 1 (January 2010). doi:10.1080/08985620903220553.

Crump, M. E. *Black Entrepreneurship: Literature and Reality*. PhD diss., Morgan State University, 2008. Baltimore.

Danes, S. M., and J. Lee. "The Effects of Ethnicity, Families and Culture on Entrepreneurial Experience: An Extension of Sustainable Family Business Theory." *Journal of Developmental Entrepreneurship* 13, no. 3 (2008): 229-68.

Disgrasian.com. "How the Vietnamese Became Salon Giants." Huffington Post. com. July 11, 2011. www. huffingtonpost.com/disgrasian/vietnamese-nail-salon_b_892773.html.

Do, A. "In Vietnamese Salons, Nails, Polish and Unvarnished Opinions." *Los Angeles Times* (Los Angeles), July 18, 2013.

Drummey, C. "2007 Industry Statistics (Vietnamese Demographics)." *Nails Big Book*, 2007. www.nailsmag.com.

Drummey, C. "First Study of Vietnamese Salon Industry Proves Some Stereotypes, Debunks Others." *NAILS*, March 2007.

Drummey, C. "Nails The Big Book." *Statistics*, 1997-2014. www.nailsmag.com.

Earth Girls Are Easy. Directed by J. Temple. Stanford, CT.: Vestron Video, 1999. Film.

Eckstein, S. "The Making and Transnationalization of an Ethnic Labour Market Niche: Vietnamese Manicurists." Lecture, 2014 International Migration Institute, Oxford Department of International Development, University of Oxford, Oxford, 2014.

Eckstein, S. "The Making and Transnationalization of an Ethnic Niche: Vietnamese Manicurists." *International Migration Review* 45, no. 3 (2011): 639-74.

Ekwulugo, F. "Gender and Entrepreneurship and SMEs in London (UK): Evaluating the Role of Black Africans in This Emergent Sector." *Journal of Management Development* 25, no. 1 (2006): 65-79.

Elam, A. B. *Gender and Entrepreneurship across 28 Countries: A Multilevel Analysis Using GEM Data*. PhD diss., University of North Carolina at Chapel Hill, 2006.

Falcon, Janine. "Mani Monday: Film Legend Tippi Hedren Receives Beauty Industry Award, Has Nail Scholarship Named in Her Honor." Beauty Geeks. September 3, 2013. http://imabeautygeek.com/2013/09/30/ tippi-hedren-receives-nail-industry-honour-and-lends-name-to-scholarship-fund/#axzz2wXAVW6TO.

Falcon, Janine. "Tippi Hedren: "Godmother of Vietnamese - American Nail Salons." Beauty Geeks. August 3, 2011. https://www.youtube.com/ watch?v=UFKhihcpxNs.

Federman, M. N., D. E. Harrington, and K. Krynski. "Vietnamese Manicurists: Are Immigrants Displacing Natives or Finding New Nails to Polish." *Industrial & Labor Relations Review* 59, no. 2 (January 2006): 302-18.

Fielden, S. L., and M. J. Davidson. *International Research Handbook on Successful Women Entrepreneurs*. Edward Elgar Publishing, 2010.

"Find an Industry Report." AnythingResearch.com. Accessed October 24, 2014. http://www.anythingresearch.com/industry/.

Finger of Doom. Directed by H. L. Pao. Shaw Brothers, 1972. VHS.

Finnan, C. R. "Community Influences on the Occupational Adaptation of Vietnamese Refugees." *Anthropological Quarterly* 55, no. 3 (1982): 161-69.

French Manicure: Tales from Vietnamese Nail Shops in America. By K. Silva, D. Nelson, and L. Folger. NPR Radio, 2007.

Gainer, N. "Florence Griffith-Joyner." Vintage Black Glamour. July 26, 2012. www.vintageblackglamour.tumblr.com/post/28087942363/olympic-icon-florence-griffith-joyner.

Gersick, K. E. *Generation to Generation: Life Cycles of the Family Business*. Harvard Business Press, 1997.

Gill, T. M. *Beauty Shop Politics: African American Women's Activism in the Beauty Industry*. University of Illinois Press, 2010.

Griffith, D., and E. Jordan. "Painted Nails a Documentary." August 2, 2013. https://www.youtube.com/watch?v=8cY-4sBQSac.

Ha, T. "The Vietnamese Nail Salon: A New Look at Ethnic Strategies in Immigrant Entrepreneurship." Speech, Annual Meeting of the American Sociological Association, Atlanta Hilton Hotel, Atlanta, GA, Atlanta, August 16, 2003.

Haines, D. W. "Binding the Generations: Household Formation Patterns among Vietnamese Refugees." *International Migration Review* 36, no. 4 (2002): 194-217.

Halkias, D., and C. Smith. *Father-Daughter Succession in Family Business: A Cross-Cultural Perspective*. Gower, 2012.

Halkias, D., P. W. Harkiolakis, and S. M. Caractsanis. *Female Immigrant Entrepreneurs: The Economic and Social Impact of a Global Phenomenon*. Gower, 2011.

Hambelton, Becky. Telephone interview by author. July 2014.

Han, J. *Eye to Eye, Nail to Nail: Body and Identity in Korean Nail Salon Workers in New York.* PhD diss., New School University, 2005. New York, 2005.

Harding, R. "Global Entrepreneurship Monitor, United Kingdom." *London Business School, London*, 2005.

Harvey, A. M. "Becoming Entrepreneurs- Intersections of Race, Class and Gender at the Black Beauty Salon." *Gender and Society* 19, no. 6 (2005): 789-808.

Hayslip, L. *When Heaven and Earth Changed Places: A Vietnamese Woman's Journey from War to Peace.* New York: Doubleday, 1989.

Heilman, M. E., and J. J. Chen. "Entrepreneurship as a Solution: The Allure of Self-employment for Women and Minorities." *Human Resource Management Review* 13, no. 2 (2003): 347--64.

History of Cosmetics.net. "Cosmetics Use in Ancient Egypt." April 2004. http://historyofcosmetics.net/cosmetic-history/ancient-egypt-cosmetics/.

Hitchcock, M., and S. Wesner. "Vietnamese Values, Networks and Family Businesses in London." *Asia Pacific Business Review* 15, no. 2 (April 2009): 265.

Hoang, H. *Culture and Management: A Study of Vietnamese Cultural Influences on Management Style.* PhD diss., Capella University, 2008.

Hoang, L. A., and B. S. A. Yeoh. "Breadwinning Wives and "Left-Behind" Husbands: Men and Masculinities in the Vietnamese Transnational Family." *Gender & Society* 25, no. 6 (December 1, 2011): 717-39.

Hofstede, G. "'Business Goals for a New World Order: Beyond Growth, Greed and Quarterly Results'" *Asia Pacific Business Review* 15, no. 4 (2009): 481-88.

Hofstede, G. *Culture's Consequences: International Differences in Work Related Values.* 2nd ed. Thousand Oaks, CA: Sage, 2001.

Hondagneu-Sotelo, P. *Domestica: Immigrant Workers Cleaning and Caring in the Shadow of Affluence.* Berkeley: University of California Press, 2001.

Huffington Post (London). "My Life: Thea Green, Founder of Nails Inc." Review of *MBE on Making It Work*, by P. Bell. November 29, 2013. http://www.huffingtonpost.co.uk/2013/11/29thea-green-nails-inc-my-life-business_n_4360652.html.

Hughes, K. D., and J. E. Jennings. *Global Women's Entrepreneurship Research: Diverse Settings, Questions, and Approaches.* Edward Elgar Publishing, 2012.

Hughes, K. "Pushed or Pulled? Women's Entry into Self-employment and Small Business Ownership." *Gender, Work & Organization* 10, no. 4 (2003).

Hunter, T. *Joy My Freedom: Southern Black Women's Lives and Labors After the Civil War.* Cambridge, MA: Harvard University Press, 1997.

Johnson, H. B. *Black Wall Street: From Riot to Renaissance in Tulsa's Historic Greenwood District.* McNay Art Museum, 1998. doi:ISBN1-57168-221-X.

Jones, C. "Oakland Looks at Trimming Number of Nail-salons." *San Francisco Chronicle*, October 7, 2009. http://www.sfgate.com/bayarea/article/Oakland-looks-at-trimming-number-0f-nail-salons-3215890.php.

Kang, M. *The Managed Hand: Race, Gender and the Body in Beauty Service Work.* Berkeley: University of California Press, 2010.

Kang, M. *Manicuring Interactions: Race, Gender and Class in New York City Korean-owned Nail Salons.* PhD diss., New York University, 2001.

Kang, S. H. *Immigrant Cultural Citizenship: Construction of a Multi-ethnic Asian American Community.* PhD diss., University of Washington, 2007. Seattle.

Kariv, D., T. Brenner, and L. Filion. "Transnational Networking and Business Performance: Ethnic Entrepreneurs in Canada." *Entrepreneurship & Regional Development* 21, no. 3 (2009).

Kelly, G. P. *From Vietnam to America, a Chronicle of the Vietnamese Immigration to the United States.* Boulder: Westview Press, 1977.

Kibria, N., C. Bowman, and M. O'Leary. *Race and Immigration.* Polity Press, 2014.

Kibria, N. *Family Tightrope, the Changing Lives of Vietnamese Americans.* Princeton: Princeton University Press, 1993.

"Kieu Chinh." Interview by K. Chinh. *Nha Magazine.* Transcript. Http://www. nhamagazine.com/back_issue/issue_0505f_p2.shtml. 1975.

Kirkwood, J. "Igniting the Entrepreneurial Spirit: Is the Role Parents Play Gendered?" *International Journal of Entrepreneurial Behavior & Research* 13, no. 1 (2007): 39-59.

Kloosterman, R., and J. Rath. *Immigrant Entrepreneurs: Venturing Abroad in the Age of Globalization.* Bloomsbury Press, 2003.

Labor and Employment Research Fund. "Intimate Labors." 2008. www.eschol-arship.org/uc/item/2cb9h7vn.

Le, Thuan. Telephone interview by author. July 2014.

Legally Blonde. Directed by R. Luketic. Hollywood, CA: MGM Studios, 2004. VHS.

Leong, T. L. "The Role of Ethnic Identity and Acculturation in the Vocational Behavior of Asian Americans: An Integrative Review." *Journal of Vocational Behavior* 44, no. W. (1994).

Leshkowich, A. M. *Tightly Woven Threads: Gender, Kinship, and "secret Agency" among Cloth and Clothing Traders in Ho Chi Minh City's Ben Thanh Market.* PhD diss., Harvard University, 2000. Boston, 2002.

Leung, K., and S. White. *Handbook of Asian Management.* Kluwer Publishers, 2004.

Levitt, P., and B. N. Jaworsky. "Transnational Migration Studies: Past Developments and Future Trends." *Annual Review of Sociology* 33, no. 129 (2007).

Lindgreen, A., and M. K. Hingley. "Challenges and Opportunities for Small and Medium-sized Populations' Arising from Ethnically, Racially and Religiously Diverse Populations." *Entrepreneurship & Regional Development* 22, no. 1 (2010): 1-4.

Lynn's Nails, Lynn. Interview by author. October 2014.

Mahler, S. J., and P. R. Pessar. "Gender Matters: Ethnographers Bring Gender From the Periphery Toward the Core of Migration Studies." *International Migration Review* 40, no. 1 (March 13, 2006): 27-63.

March, B. "Vietnamese Manicurists: The Best Nail Artists in the World." Cosmopolitan.co.uk. January 27, 2012. cosmopolitan.co.uk/beauty-hair/beauty-trends/a1318/ vietnam-hot-nail-art-beauty-backpack/#ixzz32DTtCC6x.

Marlow, S., C. Henry, and S. Carter. "Exploring the Impact of Gender upon Women's Business Ownership." *International Small Business Journal* 27, no. 2 (2009).

Mattson-Teig, B. "Regal Nails Wal-Mart: Chain Rides the Big Retailer's Coattails." *Franchise Times*, 2014. Info@franchisetimes.com.

McPherson, M. "HRM Practices and Systems within South-Asian Small Businesses." *International Journal of Entrepreneurial Behavior & Research* 14, no. 6 (2008): 414-38.

Mifflin, D. "Nail Art Creates Fingertip Renaissance." *The New York Times* (New York), July 14, 1996.

Millbun, N. "The Origin of Nail Polish." Demand Media. Accessed October 10, 2011. http://classroom.synonym.com/origin-nail-polish-9845.html.

Miller, K. "Greener Shades for Nail Salons." *Business Week*, March 5, 2007.

Morokvasic, M. "Roads to Independence: Self-employed Immigrants and Minority Women in Five European States." *International Migration* 29 (1991): 407-19.

Morris, M., and M. Schindehutte. "Entrepreneurial Values and the Ethnic Enterprise: An Examination of Six Subcultures." *Journal of Small Business Management* 43, no. 4 (October 2005).

Morrison, A., E. Schiff, and M. Sjoblom. *The International Migration of Women*. New York: World Bank and Palgrave Macmillan, 2007.

Ngo, John. Telephone interview by author. September 2014.

N.A. "A Celebration of Women™." Accessed February 8, 2009. acelebrationof-women.org.

"A Nail Story: A Nail Salon Owner Responds to the Anjelah Johnson Comedy Skit." NAILS Magazine. March 15, 2010.

http://www.nailsmag.com/ video/81539/a-salon-story.

Nail System International. "Fred Slack Jr." 2014.

www.nsinails.com/about-us/ company-history.html.

Netherton, E. N. *Identity at Their Fingertips: Language Choice and Use in Vietnamese-Owned Nail Salons*. Master's thesis, University of Texas, 2001. Auston: University of Texas.

Nguyen, D., and T. Stritikus. "Strategic Transformation: Cultural and Gender Identity Negotiation in First-Generation Vietnamese Youth." *American Educational Research Journal* 44, no. 4 (December 1, 2007): 853-95.

Nguyen, H., and N. T. Nguyen. "Examining Personal Values and Entrepreneurial Motives of Vietnamese Entrepreneurs in the 21st Century." *African and Asian Studies* 7 (2008).

Nguyen, Kien. Telephone interview by author. July 2014.

Nguyen, Monique. Telephone interview by author. July 2014.

Nguyen, Tam. Telephone interview by author. July 2014.

Nguyen, Thanh-Nghi Bao. *Vietnamese Manicurists-The Making of an Ethnic Niche*. Boston: Boston University, 2010.

Nguyen, V., and J. Rose. "Building Trust-Evidence from Vietnamese Entrepreneurs." *Journal of Business Venturiing* 24, no. 2 (March 2009): 165-82.

Nicols, B. *Buddism*. John Wiley and Sons.

doi:10:1002/9780470670590. wbeog057.

Orr, L., and W. Hauser. "A Re-Inquiry of Hofstede's Cultural Dimensions: A Call for the 21st Century Cross-cultural Research." *Marketing Management Journal* 18, no. 2 (2008).

Overland, M. A. "2 Powerful Vietnamese Women Build Private Universities." *The Chronicle of Higher Education* 55, no. 36 (February 7, 2009). Academic OneFile.

Parry, S. "Nail Salon Blues." *South China Morning Post*, September 23, 2012. Accessed October 25, 2014. http://www.scmp.com/magazines/post-magazine/article/1041471/nail-bar-blues.

Peiss, K. *Cheap Amusements: Working Women and Leisure in Turn of the Century New York*. Philadelphia: Temple University Press, 1986.

Peiss, K. *Hope in a Jar: The Making of America's Beauty Culture*. New York: Metropolitan Books, 1998.

Pham, A. "#NailedIt Documentary Trailer." April 2014. www.naileditdoc.com.

Pham, Adele, and Olivett Robinson. "Olivett Robinson Co-owner of the Nail Shop Chain "Mantrap"" Interview. 2013. Vimeo.com/7081844.

Phan, H. N. *Transnational Politics and Its Effects on the Lives of Vietnamese Americans*. Master's thesis, Northern Illinois University, 2010.

Phan, P. T. *Acculturation and the Occupational Choice of 20 Vietnamese Men*. PhD diss., University of Minnesota. 2003.

Portes, A., L. E. Guarnizo, and W. J. Haller. "Transnational Entrepreneurs: An Alternative Form of Immigrant Economic Adaptation." *American Sociological Review* 67, no. 2 (April 2002).

Prashad, V. *Everybody Was Kung Fu Fighting: Afro-Asian Connections and the Myth of Cultural Purity*. Boston: Beacon Press, 2001.

Reyes, A. *Songs of the Caged, Songs of the Free: Music and the Vietnamese Experience*. Temple University Press, 1999.

Rich, D. L. "Queen Bess: Daredevil Aviator." *Smithsonian Institute Press*, 1993, 19-21.

Rist, Yen. Telephone interview by author. July 2014.

Ross-Sheriff, F. "Globalization as a Women's Issue Revisited." *Affilia* 22 (2007): 133-37.

Rumbaut, R. G. "Children of Immigrants and Their Achievement: The Role of Family, Acculturation, Social Class, Gender, Ethnicity, and School Contexts." Proceedings of Harvard Education Inequality Seminar. www.hks. harvard.edu/inequality/Seminar/Papers/Rumbaut2.pdf.

Sanders, J. M. "Immigrant Self-Employment." *American Sociological Review* 61, no. 2 (1996): 231-49.

Shapiro, S. E. *Nails: The Story of the Modern Manicure*. Prestel Press, 2014.

Shelton, L. M., S. M. Danes, and M. Eisenman. "Role Demands, Difficulty in Managing Work-Family Conflict, and Minority Entrepreneurs." *Journal of Developmental Entrepreneurs* 13, no. 3 (2008): 315-42.

A Shot in the Dark. Directed by B. Edwards. 1964. VHS.

Sierpina, D. "Fighting for the Manicure Trade, Block by Block." *The New York Times* (New York), December 1996.

Silvey, R. "Power, Difference and Mobility: Feminist Advances in Migration Studies." *Progress in Human Geography* 28, no. 4 (August 1, 2004): 490-506.

"Stay Healthy and Safe While Giving Manicures and Pedicures: A Guide for Nail Salon Workers." Proceedings of California Healthy Nail Salon Collaborative (CHNSC) and Labor Occupational Health Program (LOHP), University of California, Berkeley. 2014. http://www.osha.gov/dte/grant_materials/fy10/ sh-20864-10/nails.pdf.

Stein, B. N. "Occupational Adjustment of Refugees: The Vietnamese in the United States." *International Migration Review* 13, no. 1 (1979): 25-45.

Sweeney, B., writer. "The Manicurist." In *The Andy Griffith Show*. Season 2. Episode 16. 1962.

Tech, L. "20/20 Nail Salon Sanitation Issue." ABC News.com. March 31, 2011. https://www.youtube.com/watch?v=8cY-4sBQSac.

Thai, M. T., and L.C. Chong. "Born Global: The Case of Four Vietnamese SMEs." *Journal of International Entrepreneurship* 6 (2008): 72-100.

Tiessen, J. H. "Individualism, Collectivism, and Entrepreneurship: A Framework for International Comparative Research." *Journal of Business Venturing* 12, no. 5 (1997): 367-84.

"Tippi Hedren the Biography." Bio. Accessed October 25, 2014. www.biography. com/people/Tippi-Hedren-9333313.

Ton, L. *Got My Nails Did*. 2010. doi:www.gotmynailsdid.com.

Toussaint-Comeau, M. "Do Ethnic Enclaves and Networks Promote Immigrant Self-employment?" *Economic Perspective 4th Quarter* 32, no. 4 (2008).

Tran, M. T. "The American Dream, One Nail at a Time." *The Seattle Times* (Seattle, WA), May 8, 2008.

Tran, N. T. *Behind the Smoke and Mirrors: The Vietnamese in California 1975-1994*. PhD diss., University of California, 2007. Berkeley: University of California Press.

Tran, T. V. "Sponsorship and Employment Status among Indochinese Refugees in the United States." *International Migration Review* 25, no. 3 (1991): 536-404.

Tseng, Y. F. "From 'us to 'them': Diasporic Linkages and Identity Politics"" *Global Studies in Culture and Power* 9 (2002): 536-50.

United States. Bureau of Labor Statistics. www.bls.gov. 2014.

United States. Department of Commerce. www.census.gov/2010census./. *2010 Census*.

United States. United Nations. Department of Economic and Social Affairs. *The World's Women 2010: Trends and Statistics*.

United States. U.S. Naval Institute and Naval History & Heritage Command 2010. *Operation Frequent Wind*. Blog ed.

"Vietnam Trade Office in the USA." Vietnam Trade Office in the USA, Languages, History, Religion and Culture. Accessed October 24, 2014. http://vietnam-ustrade.org/.

Willett, J. "Hands across the Table: A Short History of the Manicurist in the Twentieth Century." *Journal of Women's History* 17, no. 3 (Fall 2005): 59-83.

Willett, J. *Permanent Waves: The Making of the American Beauty Shop*. NY University Press, 2000, 2009.

Willoughby, I., writer. "Vietnamese Nail Salons Something of a Phenomenon in Czech Republic." In *Radio Prague*. 2009.

Wolff, R. "Salon Culture: Dzine Brings Nail Art to a New Level." ART NEWS. January 17, 2013. http://www.artnews.com/2013/01/07/ dzine-makes-nail-art-and-lowriders-and-more/.

Wood, G. T., M. J. Davidson, and S. L. Fielden. *Minorities in Entrepreneurship: An International Review*. Edward Elgar Publishing, 2012.

World Bank. "Poverty in an Age of Globalization." 2000. www.1/worldbank.org/ economicpolicy/globalization/documents/.

Wu, L. *The Effects of Ethnic Population Size on Asian Immigrant Women's Employment*. University of Maryland, College Park. January 13, 2004.

About the Author

Claudette Varnado has a Master's degree in Business Administration. Claudette is a Philosophy graduate of UC Berkeley and attended Boalt Hall School of Law. *Nail Salons* was compiled in conjunction with a post graduate research project. She resides in the Northwest.

In addition to *Nail Salons*, Claudette is the author/editor of *Love, Ben: Letters Home, the College Years 1932-1933* and *Northwest Real Estate Pro Claudette Varnado Presents Hot Tips for the First-Time Home Buyer.* Claudette is currently compiling data for a book series *SLIGHTS* about race relations in America.